Magpie

Having

Magpie

Having

Hunger
Striking

KIT BRENNAN

NUAGE
EDITIONS

Cover design by Terry Gallagher/Doowah Design.
Photograph of Kit Brennan by Andrew Willmer.
Published with the assistance of The Canada Council for the Arts.
Printed and bound in Canada by Veilleux Impression à Demande.

Canadian Cataloguing in Publication Data

Brennan, Kit, 1957–
     Magpie ; Having ; & Hunger striking

(Performance series)
Plays.
ISBN 0-921833-64-4

     I. Title.   II. Title : Having.   III. Title: Hunger striking
IV. Series: Performance series (Winnipeg, Man.)

     PS8553.R3843M34 1999   C812'.54   C99-900281-3
     PR9199.3.B6914M34 1999

Nuage Editions, P.O. Box 206, RPO Corydon, Winnipeg, MB, R3M 3S7

In loving memory of my father,
and his devotion to Canadian writing

R. E. Watters
(1912–1979)

Foreword

The three plays in this volume were written between 1992 and 1999. In preparing the manuscript for publication, I realized that they are all about characters with particular obsessions. One takes place in a rural community, one is very urban, and one wrestles with memory and myth. In each play, there are dark shadows that exist in the mind and in the body, that may become personified and all too real—shadows that tempt and call. Reality must deal with fantasy head on, and vice versa. The characters are torn between what is taboo and what is safe, between seduction and self-control. That's not to say that the plays are dark and gloomy, because they are not; one of my biggest thrills is that these plays also have moments of great humour, and that audiences laugh.

Magpie

Before moving to the prairies in 1990, I had never seen a magpie—and I had never lived in a very small town. What an extravagant, tropical-looking bird a magpie is, for such a cold climate—and what a large range of sounds it makes! As for the small town: how odd it felt to be greeted by a stranger with the words, "you're the people that painted their door bright red, aren't you?" I wasn't used to being suddenly so visible. My partner Andrew and I loved the landscape, and the sky, and the people were very welcoming, but I had no doubt: we were outsiders, observing with outside eyes. *Magpie* is a distillation of the glory and the hunger I felt all around us while living in that small town.

Having

As playwright in residence at Centaur Theatre in Montreal in 1997-98, I pitched a number of ideas to Gordon McCall, Centaur's Artistic Director (and the play's dramaturg), and the idea that became

Having is the one we were both most excited about. A play about the invasion of our homes and families by our work, about technology over simplicity, profit over romance, having over being. Our society is in a period of great extremes and of great fear. A number of years ago, when I first read Daniel Dafoe's novel *Moll Flanders,* I was struck by the parallels between those times and our own: a rising middle class whose life was ostensibly getting easier, but whose fears and rationalizations—about their own futures, their own conduct and morals—were waving in the wind. Money and accumulation of property had become the new gods, without which people could be swept away.

The highwayman of the early 18th century became a folk hero, an aristocrat of crime, and was presented to us through romantic ballads as brave and noble, worthy of our sympathy and admiration, when in fact, he robbed, raped, betrayed and often murdered. Why are we so fascinated by this hero on the stolen horse? Our heroes are often projections of what we wish we could get away with. The highwayman flourishes best in places and periods where a framework of law and order exists, but which perhaps has collapsed and no new better idea has yet taken hold, where the right of might is admired, where having is more important than living. A period much like our own?

David and Jemmy are intentionally the same age, and it is important that a sense of their linked destinies is clear by the end of the play. David is a modern equivalent, who rises and falls within the frame of the ballad. Jemmy's essence infiltrates all the characters, including Manon. Jemmy himself is a force, primarily affecting Erin in a dark and increasingly dangerous way. He also affects Olivia, who in the end is strong enough to handle him, and ready for his gift.

Hunger Striking

Why does someone stop eating, of their own free will? And why and how do they begin to eat again? I wrote *Hunger Striking* twenty years after my own experience with anorexia. Then, the condition was very unusual. Recently however, when I began to teach at a university, I fully realized how terrifyingly common it was. One day a student, struggling with her own obsession, asked me how I had recovered—and I couldn't remember. And suddenly I wanted to remember, especially how I had escaped.

The play is structured in the form of a hero journey, with classic elements such as the call to action, a mentor, an approach to the inmost cave and struggle with a dark force, as well as a resurrection/rebirth. Although the world inside an anorexic's head is a very strange place, it is not without its own logic. To outside eyes, the anorexic quest is strange and horrific, and often thought to be connected to society's and the media's obsession with thinness. In my experience, anorexia is not remotely about desiring to be beautiful. It is about power, about claiming ownership of one's life. It can be understood through journeying inside, into an understanding of the warped, anorexic logic itself. *Hunger Striking* takes an audience through the experience and out the other side, back towards life. To give up a dream and find another one that is just as compelling is painful, and when the goal is nothing less than absolute perfection—impossible to obtain if one also wants to live—the original quest must die and be replaced by something else, more earthy, more full of imperfection and forgiveness.

MAGPIE

For Andrew, with love.

Production Credits

Magpie was first produced at Twenty-Fifth Street Theatre, Saskatoon, Saskatchewan, in 1993.

Directed by Tom Bentley-Fisher
Set and Lighting design by Dan Mooney
Costume Design by Beverley Kobelsky
Choreography by Ricky Beaulieu
Music by Duane Dorgan
Stage Managed by Kathy Allen

CAST
Sharon Bakker as Bernice
Ricky Beaulieu as the Dancer
Rob Roy as Dave, Doctor and Evangelist

Magpie was First Prize Winner of the 1992 Dramatic *Grain* Contest.

I would like to acknowledge the assistance of the 1993 Banff Centre for the Arts Playwrights' Colony, under the direction of Kim McCaw. As well, Jan Selman, Jane Heather, Ken Mitchell, Sharon, Ricky (xx), Rob—and Tom, for taking a chance on me. Many thanks.

Director's Notes

Magpie was premiered at Twenty-Fifth Street Theatre in 1993 during my tenure as Artistic Director. I had just returned from a six-month sabbatical in Europe and Asia, where I was observing the work of theatres, and I was excited to be directing a play which approached its subject in such a bold and imaginative manner, similar to some of the best work I'd seen in my travels.

Kit Brennan is a playwright of tremendous depth. The play is a passionate investigation into the inner realities of Bernice, a woman trapped by the given circumstances of her life. Although it sounds a common story, Kit Brennan approaches her central character so ruthlessly, and with such insight, we feel that we have never heard the story before. It is a roller-coaster ride of emotion and confrontation that leaves its audience breathless. On the "outer," Bernice appears to be bored, submissive and uncreative. On the "inner," she is curious, daring and impassioned. We emerge at the final conclusion applauding the central character's bravery as she walks through the fire. Ms. Brennan has written a highly theatrical play which makes sense of seemingly incompatible contradictions.

Magpie is not a linear story. It takes us into an inner landscape that is not confined by time or place. It has an immediacy and complexity which challenges its audience to experience the fragments of her realities that bring her to a climax of intense destruction and personal growth.

The production at Twenty-Fifth attempted to create a world where the stakes were very high and the central character was never let off the hook—where the audience felt like voyeurs unable to disengage from the process. It incorporated various theatrical means to create the resistances required to force Bernice further and further into the dangerous unknowns in her personality. Dan

Mooney designed a set which had the effect of a bare floating island. Bernice stayed isolated on this circular platform throughout the play, with most other action occurring in a vast, dimly-lit gutter outside the circumference. The lighting design included pinpoints of illumination, emphasizing the internal aspects of the scenes rather than the given circumstances.

An important and integral aspect of the production was the use of dance. Ricky Beaulieu played the Magpie and was ever-present in Bernice's journey, dancing in and out of the action as he challenged her to inch towards freedom. Live music accompanied the production as well. A drummer, using various styles and instruments, moved and played outside the circle, forcing Bernice to listen to the voice inside her. One actor, Rob Roy, played all the men who try to keep Bernice on the straight and narrow. Again, most of his scenes were played from the surrounding circumference. Even the lighting operator was placed just outside the platform in view of the audience. All elements of the production were aggressively focused on the single task of driving Bernice into and through her fears. Often the text had the effect of being spoken barely above a whisper.

Sharon Bakker, a veteran Saskatchewan actress, played the central role and did so brilliantly. She captured the enormous richness of the character without ever overstating the obvious. She had wit and intelligence and allowed herself to play the role with honesty and vulnerability. She imploded with sexual tension. It was certainly one of the best performances we had seen in the city that season.

Kit Brennan is a bright new light in Canadian theatre. She sets up circumstances which force her characters to enter the unknown. She takes them into the fire and out the other side. I'm sure you will enjoy reading this play.

—Tom Bentley-Fisher

Staging Notes

Magpie requires three actors: one female, two male

CHARACTERS

Bernice:
A large bulky woman, 40s; obsessive personality, delusions; a somewhat nondescript appearance, but there is a great energy, a great burning inside. She is child-like, sensual and voracious, all at the same time.

The Dancer:
Male, 30s, speaks with an accent (possibly French) which sets him apart; compact and virile, generous, a teacher, at home in his body; becomes "the magpie," dancing.

The men in Bernice's life, played by same actor—

Dave:
Bernice's husband, a quiet rural man who genuinely loves Bernice and is a good father to their five children.

Doctor:
A liberal humanist who believes he is doing what is right.

Evangelist:
He has the charisma, the sexuality, the haranguing quality of the fire-and-brimstone extortioner.

Notes

A magpie is a noisy, black and white bird with a long tail and short wings, related to the jays; a mostly solitary bird who likes to steal bright, shiny objects; a talented imitator of other birds' calls. Also colloquial for a person who chatters.

An evocative score which underpins the exterior and interior landscapes is crucial to production. During the evangelical meetings, the swelling, throbbing of the congregation's rising excitation should be evident. The first production of the play was underscored by percussion drumming.

The Dancer's training is more jazz/ballroom than balletic. He is everything Bernice aspires to be and that her background rejects as frivolous. The dances, like the scoring, should be evocative rather than literal, and sometimes in counterpoint to Bernice's words. The Dancer's dances (as a man) should be profoundly different from those of the magpie.

As the magpie, the Dancer is both the inner Bernice, self-mutilated—and the gorgeously arrayed, flamboyant life force that eludes her and drives her.

Bernice's memories of the magpie are filled with tension, a deeply buried source of pain; sexuality, great cruelty and the lost innocence of a child.

The play takes place in the here and now, on the day Bernice is to go home from convalescence, and also in memory: the long past and the recent past. The feeling of outer reality/inner reality, past and present, should be established early. Bernice slips in and out freely. In the opening, it is important that the shift from Dave to Doctor to Dave to Evangelist is subtle but takes place in clear view of the audience; after this, the shifts may be less overt.

Magpie

The Dancer is curled up on the floor.

Bernice enters, lumpy; she is carrying articles to be packed. She sees Dancer, stops. Ignores him, goes around him. Looks back. Turns away. Looks back.

Dave appears, sitting outside Bernice's room, cap in hands.

Bernice inches towards Dancer, trying to coax it.

Dave clears his throat.

Bernice moves away from Dancer, turns her back to him her eyes dead, her hands busy.

The Dancer begins to move. He rises, arms upraised, on one leg. He spreads his wings, yearning upwards.

Bernice does not look toward the Dancer.

Bernice: *(Whispered, prayed; from hopelessness to excitement, rising through the following.)* And then I said to him, I said "I never meant for you to think that. I'd do anything to make you happy, I swear to God, and how could you possibly want to break my heart like this when you know how much I love you?" That's what I said. And he, he cried with joy to hear those words from my mouth, pouring out of my mouth. It was beautiful. Truly beautiful. And we collapsed backwards onto his couch, and he took me then and there, and the door was closed, and no one saw, but I saw, I was there. And the Lord God saw that it was good. It was so good!

She sees the audience. The Dancer arrests in mid-flight.

I'm just kidding.

The Dancer curls into the floor.

What? I'm just telling a tale! Don't get me wrong, ok?
It's just a tale told by an idiot, signifying nothing, right?
I bin to school; went back, did night classes, English lit
and that. I know that stuff, eh?

I'm just kidding around.

*She laughs loudly, stops short; the Doctor appears, looks
at his watch, looks in at her—she's aware of him, but
does not look at him.*

Doctor: Bernice?

Bernice: What?

Doctor: How are you doing in there?

Bernice: Good.

Doctor: Fine. No rush. Let me know if I can help.

Bernice: Oh, I will.

Doctor: Another five minutes?

Bernice: 'Bout that.

Doctor: ...Right. I'll come for you.

He exits.

Bernice: *(To audience.)* What are you looking at?

Tell you something I just figured out. So help me God, I
never knew this before. Listen, maybe this'll help you,
you know, you can avoid the heartache I bin through.
Listen.

If you have life and energy in you, they want it. They want it so much they'll do anything to rip it out of you. They will. There. You can have that for nothing. Tell that to your kids some dark stormy night, and don't let them tell you you never gave them nothing.

> *Dave coughs, fiddles with his cap. She's aware of this sound.*

(*To audience.*) Bet you thought you'd landed in some sort of loony bin, eh? Here's this woman, talking to herself. Chatting away, just chatting and telling tales. But don't you believe it.

It's like I tell my kids, all five of them bright and shiny as new pins—I tell them, you go to school and read books and do what they tell you and you'll go far. You will. Long as you do what they say.

> *The Dancer begins to rise, as Dave becomes Evangelist.*

My life and that's given me this gift, oh yes. I'm here before you, the multitudes. On the air. On the air we reach the people, on the air is freedom. And the time is running out! I found that out for sure and ever, I found that out, you know. Well, you can see! And so I'm here to tell you, you in the studio and you in your living rooms there, I'm here to tell you the time is now, the time is writ and burnished in gold! And the face of the world is gonna be changed! You gotta make a change!

> *The Evangelist appears, in her head. The Dancer becomes immobile, out of the range of the Evangelist's gaze.*

Evangelist: Oh, no, Bernice, no, no.

> *Bernice freezes.*

Bernice: …What was I saying? (*Carefully.*) I've been resting, eh? I been taking on too much, I always do that. And I've got to be careful. If I don't, I'm gonna die. I will.

The Evangelist fades away. She waits, then:

See this dress? He gave it to me. 'Cause he thinks I'm so
beautiful, he got it for me and no one else in the whole
world has a dress like this. No one. It's one of a kind, like
me. That's what he says. I'm not making it up. He tells
me embarrassing stuff like that and I say Shh! what are
people going to think, you talking to me like that and
you my teacher? They don't like that. They don't like
that kind of life and love going on right under their
noses, you know. They'll say anything to stop it. 'Cause
they're afraid. They're afraid of it.

The Dancer begins, carefully, to strut.

And I've got to be careful, so careful. 'Cause I'm
delicate. That's what he tells me. He says, "You're so
delicate, Bernice. You're just like a little china figurine.
If I was to put you on one of those things that go round,
like on a music box, you know, with the snow and the
glass bubble and that, why then I'd put you way up high
where no one could come along and knock you off by
accident. No one could whoops with their elbow and
make you fall and spill your waters all over the floor,
and break you into little pieces no way. No more." And
God said Let the waters under the heaven be gathered
into one place, and let the dry *land* appear, and it was so.
And it was me. I appeared. And he saw that it was good.

She covers her mouth.

Oh, shit. There I go. I'm doing it again. Those words,
they keep coming out of my mouth. Toads. Bunch of
toads. Falling out.

Looks around to be sure she's not being watched.

But I'm just a silly. That's what my ma used to say.
"You're just a big silly, Bernice. What are you going on
about now?" She'd be so exasperated with me, and I'd
laugh!

She follows the dancer with her eyes.

"You live in your head, Bernice." That's what she'd say. "You just get down to business, girl. That'll stand you in good stead." Steady. Steady on. Steadfast and that. The steadfast tin soldier, standing on his one leg, looking at his love. The china ballerina with a missing leg, just like his. But it isn't missing, see? That's the thing—it's just hid, up under her skirt. He just can't see it. So she isn't like him. He's all alone. Falls into the fire, nobody notices him; melted and missing parts, thrown out with the ash, shit on by dogs—(oops, pardon my French)— he sails off down this sewer pipe, longing for his ballerina, longing for his one true love. But she's whole and he's not, and he doesn't even know. Into the dark and the stench, out of the light of the world, not one word of blame, not one shout of "!" *(Inarticulated rage chokes her.)*

My kids don't like that one. And I don't blame them. There's no happy ending.

Picking up, fondling clothes.

When I was a girl, I'd go tramping off round the farm. We had a big farm. It's out near Stony Bend in Saskatchewan and my dad, he raised cattle mostly, coupla pigs. He kept us at it. I'd take a book—I love to read, I've always loved it, even in high school when you're not supposed to be interested in books, you know, but in boys?—I'd take a book, a romance like or something with a lot of colour. This book'd be under my arm, and I'd take off in the spring in my rubber boots, and go walking. I'd be out for hours, rip off a piece from the wolf willows, pretend I was in a movie, you know. I'm smoking this twig all elegant, like Lauren Bacall or Ingrid Bergman in one of those old black and white films... I wanted a trench coat so bad and my dad said "Don't be stupid. How you going to milk the cows in one of those things?" ...Anyway, there I'd be, each part of the picture I'm in unreeling before me, around me, in me, scene by scene: a captured maiden, a foreign spy, dark deeds and that. I can see them all. I'd park myself under a tree and I'd read and read, and I'd get so, oh, I'd get so into that book, I'd get so restless and I'd get so wet, I— ...Anyway, they'd call for me, and I wouldn't hear them. Or maybe I'd be walking back home. I'd be walking and they'd call for me and I'd look at them and think, who are they talking to? I'd never recognize them. And they'd get so mad! My ma'd shake her head. And my dad'd shake me. But I've always needed that, eh?

The Doctor enters Bernice's room.

Doctor: Bernice.

The Dancer slips behind, then shadows the Doctor.

Bernice: Ooops. I'm almost done! I just—some things got put away wrong, that's all. I'm just fixing them.

Doctor: Take your time.

Bernice: I will. I've been resting, so I'm not used to rushing, eh?

Doctor: I wanted to make sure you have everything you need.

Bernice: I do. It's all here.

Doctor: Good.

He glances at his watch.

Bernice: Um... Doctor?

Doctor: Mm?

Bernice: ...Nothing.

Turning, the Doctor is frozen in time; the Dancer attempts to fly away, but is rooted to the ground.

(*Caressing the Dancer's body.*) There's this place I know, this place in the park, under the statue; the wind doesn't get in there, nor the sun, just the darkness, and it's damp and warm. I lie back and I feel you, I feel your hands running down my body, I feel your need of me and it frightens me because I'm too small for you. You'll hurt me, you'll bruise me, you'll break my bones and crush me under you. I'm delicate and fragile and I'm wet, I'm so wet under you where it's warm and damp and dark. And I'm—uh!

She feels inside her clothing, excited, ashamed, wet. The Dancer, released, dances away from her. Time resumes.

...I've been resting.

Doctor: That's good, Bernice. Very good.

The Doctor exits; the Dancer slips out behind him and is gone.

She yanks out all of the packed clothing and begins again, folding, sorting, aware of the Dancer's desertion.

Bernice: They've got their eyes on me. All of them do, and I know why. They can't stand it when one of us gets out, gets away from them, escapes!

They say I live in my head. Well, so? So do other creative people, so I don't see how that can be bad. Inside, I'm an artist. I'm creating all the time, all the time. They won't let me watch the soaps, and I love those shows, eh? And what's more, so does half the entire population of the North American continent, and half that audience is men sneaking in to get a daily dose of the lives of their favourites, right? To know what's going to happen next, to know what's going to *happen!*

I miss those shows. They don't want me watching so much TV.

But what else am I going to do, eh? Got any ideas? I tell you, without TV, most women would go stark raving mad. I got ideas. I got ideas flying around my head all the time, but ideas mean money. You got to have money, your *own* money, to make ideas come true. And don't lie to me and tell me that's a load of shit, because every idea I've ever had, it's been shot down by someone saying to me, you got your registration fee? You got your membership fee? You got your student card? You got your Tupperware, you got your wedding band, you got your kids! And if you think that all doesn't cost big money, then you're nuts. You want to have ideas, you better be ready to pay for them!

Hey. You didn't come here for this kind of talk and who the hell am I, right? I'm sorry.

(Nods toward the Doctor.) He's probably going to give me hell, anyway. Stick around, you can watch that. *There's* something you can get your teeth into. Conflict, pure and simple. Sure, I know, I'm not stupid. The six o'clock news, the police car down the street, the blood on the highway and we slow past, gawking. It's what we live for.

Waiting for something to happen.

He hates it when I get loud, when I get mad and that. They all do. They don't want to go there with me. But things just swell up, get red and sore, and how you gonna let them burst—you take away the soaps, you take away the romance and that—where's it gonna go? Eh? That's what they can't tell me, all their fancy words—that's the little hole in the logic the water slips through, the hole in the sock the big toe wiggles out of. Oh, yes, there's a hole. Bigger all the time. And it's in me. In ME! So!

(Small.) ...Come back...

Hey! I love ideas, eh? I love the way they pop, little explosions, like microwave popcorn, bursting around inside. All contained in your head. Nobody can see them if you don't want them to. They're just *there.*

They're sustaining, you know. Nurturing. Nobody can take them away.

Stops what she's doing.

I know what you're thinking. I can see it, I can feel it. How come this woman's using these big words— sustaining, nurturing? She's from Saskatchewan. Oh, I see it. Pretty good, eh, seeing inside your heads? Well, you know what? Bullshit. Bull shit! I bin around. My eyes are open. Who the hell do you think you are? Just who the hell!

The Doctor appears.

Doctor: Bernice.

Bernice: What?

Doctor: How are you doing? Hm?

Bernice: I'm doing good.

Doctor: Your husband is here. You remember?

Bernice looks hunted.

Bernice: Who?

Doctor: Dave. He's come to take you home. You're almost ready?

Bernice: Almost. Soon.

Doctor: I know you're feeling uncertain about this, Bernice. But you remember what we talked about?

Bernice: When?

Doctor: This morning. Remember, this morning we decided— one step at a time? One step, leads to the next, to the next. And so we build up confidence.

Bernice: …I don't know.

Doctor: One task completed. And what was that?—you remember?

Bernice: Sure I do.

Doctor: ...Yes?

Bernice: Get up in the morning.

Doctor: And?

Bernice: ...I don't know.

Doctor: Make sure your kids get a good breakfast. Before they leave for school. Remember?

           She nods.

           And so you're on your way. Each day. A step at a time. Now. Can I help you with anything?

Bernice: No! I mean, I'm fine. For now.

Doctor: He's been very patient, Dave. Very understanding.

Bernice: Ok, but I'm just—wait!

Doctor: ...With you?

Bernice: No, just—outside. Just outside.

           He turns, becomes Dave.

           I know, you know.

           But what else am I gonna do? Eh? How else am I gonna...

           (Re: Dave) I see him there. Bin there all the time, waiting. You see him too, don't you?

           I'm not ready for that. Not ready.

           Bernice and Dave speak the following simultaneously.

Bernice: *(Packing everything neatly.)* Forgive me, Father, for I have sinned. I have committed abomination with my mouth, and I am without grace. I have done it all, every whisper, every dark and secret thing. Under the statue. And other places. Other places. On the air, on the wing, I have done it all, I swear to God. And I come to you, Father, to be—

Dave: *(To Doctor.)* When you told me she'd do well coming here I thought, what'll I do without Bernie? Coming in the door and the place all steamed up from the dishes and the heat she keeps the place at. The bills are high, but she complains about the cold. I figure it's worth it. And the little one just out of diapers. I thought, what am I supposed to do, Bern?

Bernice: *(Solo.)* —healed by your mouth. By the laying on of hands.

Dave: I don't know what happened…

Bernice: By the laying *on*. Other places…

Dave: When I come here, I got two left feet, and… Well, I wondered. Don't know if this restin's so good for her. Just give her time to get worked up.

           Dave and Bernice speak the following simultaneously.

Bernice: Lay *on* me, Lord. Heavy, heavy—

Dave: Keep me busy, that's all the medicine *I* need.

           Dave disappears.

Bernice: *(Solo.)*—getting off the ground.

           Her packing is done.

           Whether I'm the hero of my own life, or whether that place is taken by someone else, these pages must show. *David Copperfield.* Grade 11.

Who else would be occupying that place if not me?
That's what I want to know.

(A yell at the prairie sky.) Who else could it be!

Out on the farm... It'uz beautiful. There's God in that
sky. Oh, I know, another prairie flower ranting on about
the sky and that. But every cliché comes from about a
million truths that've made it a reality, right? "Your
cheating heart," or "a face that launched a thousand
ships"—Helen o' Troy, she caused the whole Trojan
War, eh? But, ok, the sky. I live in the city now, small
city. Well, not even that. It's a town, if you must know.
But it doesn't feel the same in town. There's no God in
that sky. There's no God anywhere.

I spent so long looking for him, for God. He tucks
himself away, he giggles in corners, he plays tricks. I
used to worry myself sick about what he wanted, you
know what he wanted me to do with myself, why I was
put here, what I was supposed to *do*. We'd go to church
every Sunday, all of us kids and my dad and ma. I'd be
looking around (get a swat too if I wasn't careful). I'd
look and try and see inside those others, sitting there,
half asleep; one old guy in front of us every Sunday
farting, all uncomfortable, and we'd bust ourselves
trying not to laugh and ma'd look disgusted, at us or at
the smell she never would say. They none of them
seemed concerned at the things the preacher said, but
it'd freeze the blood in my bones—all the things I
should and shouldn't do. My dad'd give me a wallop
for "dreaming" he called it, when I was just trying to
work it through.

I'd watch the Roman Catholics, off to their cathedral.
My friend Bonnie's an RC, took me in there one time
when we were fifteen, all secret like or Ma'd kill me. St.
Mary's. The Holy Virgin. The smell, the dark. The
priest's robes and that. I thought it was amazing, I was
so jealous. Bonnie could tell her innermost things, she
could tell them in the dark. 'Course she said she never

did. It was always little things like mean thoughts or skipped homework and I'd say *why*, Bonn? I wouldn't waste it. If I were her.

My ma'd say there's no need to dwell on the dark. You're the oldest, Bernice. I'm counting on you. Take care of your brothers, and don't be a silly. The big box of Kotex in her bedroom closet—what's that, Ma? You'll find out soon enough. Like a sentence. Like a threat. None of *them* felt that, my brothers. They thought it was funny. Because they were scared. Because they had something on me. Something filthy. In the dark all the time, all the time.

She hesitates. This is difficult.

…There was this magpie. On the farm. He lived around the pine trees down by the mail box. Never seemed to have a mate, just flew around by himself. Stayed all winter too—in Saskatchewan! Crazy bird!

Some mornings my brothers and I we'd go hurtling over to the barn, it was so damn cold the snot would freeze in your nose, and I'd be milking and thinking of that bird. Out there all alone.

(*Coaxing.*) Do you drink milk? And my dad'd say, "Don't be an idjit. It's a damn bird!"

The Dancer appears, summoned, cautious.

Why does it have such a long, beautiful tail, Dad? Why it and none of the other birds?

Then Dad swats me, 'cause he doesn't know the answer, eh? We always try to make him believe he knows everything, else he gets pissed off, and once we got the hang of it we never asked questions we figgered he wouldn't know the answer to.

C'mere, bird, hey?

Doctor: *(Calls.)* Bernice. He's here.

Bernice: *(Startled.)* Who?

>   *Dave enters; the Dancer becomes immobile.*

Dave: Now then, Bernie.

>   *Pause.*

Bernice: …You bin getting enough to eat?

Dave: Your mother's been out. Staying with us.

Bernice: She cooking good things?

Dave: Good enough. We miss you, though. Glad you'll be coming home.

>   *Cautious, the Dancer preens; very subtle, through the following, unconsciously distracting Bernice.*

Bernice: I bin having problems keeping things down again. I don't know if I'm ready.

Dave: They said—

Bernice: I know what they said, but I'm telling you I don't know if I'm ready yet. That's all.

Dave: Oh.

Bernice: So. Can she stay on?

Dave: Who?

Bernice: My mother!

Dave: Well, I don't know. She was staying tonight. She wants to see you…

Bernice: I don't want to see her.

Dave: Bernice. Don't say that, now. She's your mother.

Pause.

Dave: So what do you want me to do?

Bernice: I have an eating disorder, can't keep nothing down.
          They told you, didn't they? I'm under a lot of stress.
          How am I supposed to cope with you all? Running
          around dropping food all over the kitchen floor. It
          drives me to drink, honest to God, Dave! It drives me to
          drink.

Dave: Oh, now—

Bernice: I'm bound to up and die, man. You don't have any idea
          what I've been going through, not any idea! I can't go
          back there yet. I'm frightened. I'll fall apart. I will. Tell
          them that.

Dave: Oh, Bernie.

Bernice: I will. I'm not kidding.

          He goes, sits with his head in his hands.

          *Freed, the Dancer struts and flies. Bernice yearns for
          him.*

Bernice: Oh… I always wanted to fly. Always. I was made for
          flight.

          It's this eating disorder, that's what the problem is. I
          can't eat. I get so thin I can't get off the ground, I'm too
          weak. I eat like a bird, can't keep nothing down. He told
          me, he said, you've *got* to eat, Bernice. You're too thin.
          You're going to blow away in the next big wind. And I
          laughed and said don't worry about me, I'll be fine, and
          he said to me, he said, me not worry? You're all I think
          about. You're what I live for, you are. You're my
          princess in her ivory tower, on her glass mountain, in
          her copper castle. You're my china figurine. That's the
          kind of things he says, my teacher. He's my dancing
          teacher. He loves me true. He does. No matter what they
          say, I believe in him. He'd never forsake me. Never.

Come back! Come back, come back, come back!

The Dancer pauses over Dave.

Dave: *(To the Doctor.)* I don't know what you're telling her about this eating disorder thing here, but she's no more disordered'n me! She eats as much as me. Always was a healthy eater, always will be! I just want to bring her home. I want her to come back. The kids sure miss her. They surely do.

Dave disappears, with the Dancer.

Bernice: Come back…

She pulls out a bag of potato chips, eats mechanically.

That man that came earlier? That Dave? He's just a man I buy food for. I don't know him. He lives in a trailer park. There's this little kitchen and a tiny refrigerator, and he expects me to put food on the table for him and five kids. Five! Where they all came from I couldn't tell you.

Oh, yes, they're mine. They're mine, all right. I just don't remember what led up to their arrival. You must think I'm lying to you, but honest to God, it's that forgettable. I remember the feeling inside, I remember them growing and the way my body felt, I remember their births, the first's head all lumpy from the forceps, my last one slipping out like a seal—those things I remember like it was yesterday, each one of them separate. But him. Him I don't recall.

I'm not ready for that. I've told them. I can't keep nothing down.

I walk up and down the aisles. I put food in the basket. I figure out what to make. I pay with his money. I'm forced to serve them, you know. It's like my penance, but all the time I know some day soon, some beautiful morning, they're going to wake up and I won't be there any more. *He* will have taken me away. He's coming

and they'd better get used to it because the face of the
world is going to be changed. And it's a strain, knowing
and never telling, never letting on the things you *know*
inside are about to happen, never letting even the tiniest
little explosion of joy and expectation escape your lips
because they're jealous and they'll try to stop you.They
can't stand to see true love, true sexuality. They can't
stand it.

She crumples the empty bag, hides it unconsciously.

Born and bred Presbyterian, eh? But there you go. I got
an open mind. I like to know what's going on, what
other people think. My ma'd die'f she knew. You're the
only girl, Bernice. We got to keep them going right. We
got to keep the faith. What'll people think, you not there
every Sunday? *They're* not going! How come I got to go!
I been away from home over half my life—funny how
the years go. How she keeps her hold. Never kept it over
my brothers, drinkin' and swearin'. Just goes to show.

...Anyway. One summer night, just after my third, I
went to a revivalist. I did. You don't believe me?
Something to do, like, see what all the fuss was. See, my
friend Cheryl was always going on about him, the
preacher; said he was a wonderful man, he'd make you
feel so pure and that. She got me curious. And I was—
well, I wasn't feeling so good, you know. And anyway.
This preacher, I knew him to see him, through the
Legion, eh? Where my dad went. He's been around,
municipal politics and that, well respected family man.
Good head of silver hair. Lots of women going and the
husbands didn't mind. He had a hall, a big crowd of
people went every Sunday. She said, Cheryl said, it was
like a well kept secret, it was a beautiful sacred place.
She's like me, Cheryl—three little kids, one of them not
out of diapers. Well, I got two more now, but this was
three years ago, eh? And we get along all right, her and
me, watch the soaps together sometimes, though I'd
rather watch them on my own than gabbing away and
wondering what I'd missed and that. Anyway, there I

was, middle of the summer, baking in this hall with the windows closed like we were doing something we shouldn't be. My ma woulda killed me! She was all excited, Cheryl, her face all red and shining—

Music begins under, swelling.

Evangelist: Woe to Ariel, to Ariel, the city where David dwelt! And I will camp against thee round about, and will lay siege against thee with a mount, and I will raise forts against thee.

Under, sound of congregation grows, ecstatic and fervent.

(He continues low under Bernice's following speech.) And thou shalt be brought down, and shalt speak out of the ground, and thy speech shall be low out of the dust, and thy voice shall be as of one that hath a familiar spirit, out of the ground, and thy speech shall whisper out of the dust. Thou shalt be visited of the Lord of hosts with thunder, and with earthquake and great noise—

Bernice: Well, I'd heard of this, eh? But I'd never seen it. And the music, and the singing. And the heat; it was so hot. And his suit, well, he was moving. He was working so hard, for us, for all of us. And I looked about me and I thought, look at that. Look at what they're doing. Why them and not me? Why are they falling down and not me? They're no better than me. They're my neighbours. And that's the auctioneer over there. I just saw him doing his thing last Friday. He's no better than me. What do they hear that I don't?

Evangelist: *(Solo.)*—with storm and tempest, and the flame of devouring fire!

Bernice: I looked at him and I just thought—he's gonna burst into flame!

Evangelist: *(Under Bernice's following speech.)* And the multitude of all the nations that fight against Ariel, and that distress her, shall be as a dream of a night vision. It shall even be as when an hungry man dreameth, and behold, he eateth; but he awaketh, and his soul is empty: or as when a thirsty man dreameth, and, behold, he drinketh: but he awaketh, and, behold, he is faint, and his soul hath appetite.

Bernice: And then I began to figure it out, you know. They all *wanted* to speak in tongues. They wanted it and that's why they'd come. He'd walk among them, and lay his hand on their heads, and they'd fall back and they were flying, they were! They were flying down there on the ground! And Cheryl was fallen on the ground too. She was wiggling and almost frothing at the mouth. You know, part of me was saying this is ludicrous, Bernice. You get on out of here and never come back—

(Solo.)—but part of me—*(She opens her mouth and a magpie croak falls out.)*

Evangelist: Stay yourselves, and wonder! cry ye out, and cry!—

Crescendo.

—they are drunken, but not with wine; they stagger, but not with strong drink!

The congregation comes to rest, ecstatic. Bernice looks around, frantic, pretends to experience ecstasy, and falls down.

For the Lord hath poured out upon you the spirit of deep sleep, and hath closed your eyes. Peace be with you. We shall pass among you for your offering.

Bernice alone, a harsh revealing light.

Bernice: *(Shamed.)* Well, I…

Why'd you stay for that part? Shoulda gone out for popcorn. Bathroom break. Why'd you stay to see?

…So, anyway.

I only wanted what they had.

Pause.

She struggles to her feet and follows the Evangelist.

Bernice: Excuse me. I couldn't help it. I was moved by what you were saying.

Evangelist: Of course.

Bernice: That part about being hungry, and being filled. I... Can you go over that again for me? I mean... I want to understand.

Evangelist: This is your first time?

Bernice: Yes, it is.

Evangelist: Well, scripture goes on to remind us: shall the work say of him that made it, He made me not? You see?

Bernice: You mean we...? No, Father.

Evangelist: No need to call me Father, child. We don't have that wall between us. Think of it this way. You have been created in the image of God. All of you, every hair and follicle. All your secrets are known to Him. Loved by Him.

Bernice: Loved?

Evangelist: Truly. Look to Isaiah 29. Seek and ye shall find. But don't seek too hard. Let it come to you.

Bernice: But...my life...there's more...

Evangelist: Come again. You will feel it.

Bernice: I feel nothing!

Evangelist: Trust me. It will come.

Bernice: I—

Evangelist: Woe unto them that seek to hide their counsel from the Lord, and are in the dark, and doubt, saying, Who seeth us? Who knoweth us? Come again, child, and find release. Excuse me.

Bernice: Who seeth me? Who knoweth me? That's just what I want to know! I don't want to hide, I'm *made* to hide! Feel nothing! Cut off!

I went again. *(Following him.)* And again— I'll leave my husband!

Evangelist: No, no, Bernice. You have been joined to him. You bear his children. No, no.

He moves on.

Bernice: He'd pass us in the streets as if he never caused such burning. Or in the supermarket. In the frozen foods. Cut up. In parcels. Here we feel, here we don't. I'm empty! I go on Sunday. I go alone. I think of him. I pray. I pray. I go, I go, I have to go. Three years. Each week, I think, that was it, I felt it. But then inside, a NO!

They're all pretending, they must be!

And then—

The Dancer and the Evangelist meet in a public place. Bernice edges closer to their conversation; they don't notice her.

Evangelist: Settling in?

Dancer: I begin to be.

Bernice: I just stopped dead.

Evangelist: All fixed up in your place now?

Dancer: Just the mirrors to come.

Bernice: I seen him on the TV.

Evangelist: That's one thing I've never understood about this dance business—but the consultants told us it was *doo riggur,* that the right word?

Dancer: *(Smiling.)* That's it, more or less.

           They laugh.

Bernice: Something about him. And my preacher, so sour.

Evangelist: Piano playing's good enough for me, but the other committee members said—no, dance.

Dancer: Well, I'm glad for that, yes? Most college programs have all but dance—music, painting, those ones come first. But dance? Pff. Left out.

Evangelist: Not our town.

Dancer: And you are with the Board of Governors?

Evangelist: Some of us have to keep an eye on the money, eh, young man?

Dancer: But, yes. I'm pleased to meet you.

           They shake hands.

Evangelist: Sure, it's good for the little ones, all that moving around, but for us big people—well, how can you stand to stare at yourself all the time, hm? Pretty vain I call it.

Dancer: Do you? Seeing the outside helps us look within. To straighten the spine, contact the points of pain. To see— straight.

           They assess each other.

Evangelist: Well, good luck to you.

Dancer: Thank you.

           They move apart. Bernice fixes on the Dancer.

Bernice: Contact the points of pain. Who seeth me straight.

            She turns to Dave.

            I need some money for a class.

Dave: What's that, Bern?

Bernice: I want to do a class in town. Over on 52nd.

Dave: What kind of class?

Bernice: Dancing and that.

Dave: Dancing, Bern? Where we off to, the Riviera?

Bernice: Don't, it's not a—

Dave: What put this idea in your head?

Bernice: It was on the TV. Last weekend. And then I saw—I want
            to do it.

Dave: Hey, I like you just the way you are.

Bernice: *(Angry.)* I want to do it, I want to go, I want to do this
            class!

Dave: Ok, Bern, ok. Things are kind of tight, old girl, but we'll
            see what we can do, hm? Come on, don't sulk. How
            much is it?

Bernice: I'll use the baby bonus.

Dave: I don't think—

Bernice: It's my money, it's what I'm paid! It's all I've got that's
            mine! All right!

            Dave sighs, shakes his head, exits.

            That's right. That's right…

            Oh, no. No, no…

Fixed on the Dancer, she now approaches him, frightened.

…I got close to one once—a magpie. He was busy pulling at a worm, tugging and tugging. I remember how beautiful he was up close, so black and shiny, with that white white chest, and green and blue glossy in his tail and his wings.

He never saw me. He was too busy, too occupied. He didn't notice me, though I was bigger than him. I'm small, I'm light on my feet, but I *am* a human being and he's just a bird, ok? I got close. He never knew. He never knew a thing. His back was to me, and—

Dancer: *(Turns.)*.Oh, hello. Can I help you?

Bernice is shy, bumbling; a new reality, this day in her past.

Bernice: Is this—is this where you sign up for the dance classes?

Dancer: Why, yes, it is.

Bernice: I thought I was in the wrong place. Sorry for stepping on your…

Dancer: That's all right, no harm done. How did you hear about the studio?

Bernice: It was on the TV.

Dancer: Ah, good! Those ads cost a fortune. Television's the way to go, hm?

Bernice: I saw *you* on TV.

Dancer: *(Laughs.)* Don't remind me.

Bernice: And other places… Other places.

Pause.

Dancer: So. When are you free to come, and what kind of classes would you like?

Bernice: Oh, I— I don't know. I just saw the ad and...

Dancer: Have you ever taken classes before?

Bernice: Well, no, I—there's never been a place here before. Just the step dance and that, at school. High school, you know.

Dancer: Sure. What made the college decide to start a dance program?

Bernice: Oh, I—

Dancer: People like you, a wish for the arts?

Bernice: ...I wouldn't know about that.

Dancer: No? I was surprised—a well-advertised position for such a small town, wanted to know the background, you know?... *(Sensing her nervousness.)* Well, what interests you? Aerobics? Ballet? Jazz?

Bernice: ...Do you have others like me? Taking ballet? Or is it all kids? See, I'm not sure, I—

Dancer: There are other women, don't worry. You won't be alone.

Bernice: Oh, good.

Dancer: Ah, I see. You were worried it would be just you and me, yes? Too much attention, too many things to remember all at once?

Bernice: *(Laughs.)* I guess.

Dancer: Or just one lonely adult in a sea of little children. That's it, yes?

She nods.

Well you see, I'm not a monster. I'm just a man. Like all the rest.

Bernice: No.

Dancer: No? I'm not a man?

Bernice: *(Flustered.)* No, I mean... Not like all the rest.

Dancer: Ah, she's found me out. So soon, too. Oh la la.

Bernice laughs.

Bon. That's good, laughter. A good sign. So. How often do you want to come? Once a week, or twice?

Bernice: I—twice! That is, if the others—

Dancer: I've been urging everyone to come twice a week if they can. It will be fine.

Bernice's memory begins to edit and enhance her role.

(Writing.) Your name?

Bernice: Bernice. Marshall.

Dancer: Do you want to pay monthly or weekly?

Bernice: Um... Monthly.

Dancer: Cash or cheque?

Bernice: Cheque.

Dancer: Fine.

Bernice: What should I wear?

Dancer: Oh, loose things. To begin. Things that can really move. And then we'll see, ok?

Bernice: ...Ok.

Dancer: *(He smiles.)* Well, then. Tuesday at 7:00 to begin, all right?

Bernice: You're not from around here, are you?

Dancer: No.

Bernice: You talk sort of funny—oh, I don't mean that. It's just
           that you don't sound the way we do. It's—

Dancer: You mean I have an accent?

Bernice: Yes.

Dancer: You won't hold that against me, will you? All of you? I
           mean, to *me*, it's *you* who have the accent. Yes?

Bernice: Yes.

> *The Dancer turns away. She moves slowly, dreamily.*

That's the way he talked. Right from the start. You see
what I mean. How could I resist him, my dancer? I'd
never known anyone like him, except on the screen. But
up close—oh—he's tall and dark and dresses like a
prince. He has long legs. I focus on his legs. They're
beautiful. The long, long thighs, the things he wears, the
way he sweats by the end of the class and the things he
says. It's like a secret language. I know it's for me and
me alone. He can't hide the way he feels. It's in his face
and it's there, visible. It's there in the meeting place
between his—

> *She stops suddenly, looks away from him.*

No! That's wrong. Toads keep falling, falling out. He's
small, he speaks funny, he waves his hands around a lot
when he's talking and he lets his hair grow long. And he
wears—he has—he wears an earring! Oh, I know they
do that all over. Lots of the TV stars have them in real
life but don't wear them on camera, and it doesn't mean
he's queer or anything like that. I know that. I'm not
stupid. I'm not just some hick that knows nothing! But
he's—he's different. He…disturbs me… He creeps into
my dreams and I feel his hands slipping up my thighs.
I—

Dave: *(Entering.)* What's for supper, Bern?

Bernice: …What?

Dave: Old belly's doing a jig here. Had me out on a job today, way down in Biggar. Now, there's a sight—the face on some poor gaffer when his new rig pulls off the highway, coming up his drive. Dream come true. Air-conditioned, headphones, the works—and the guy's fields are simply blowing away. Blowing into Montana. Whew. What's this country comin to? Eh, girl?

Bernice: Get off.

Dave: Hey? What're we comin to?

Bernice: Your hands are filthy. Messin' me up. Go on and wash.

> *He does. The Dancer moves past.*

I told him I couldn't dance, eh? That was a toad. I've been dancing ever since I was born. It's the only thing I was made for. I had to dance. No one would stop me. And that's a diamond. Toads and diamonds, sort them out.

I went twice a week, twice a week from then on. All last winter, snow or sleet, I'd get there somehow, never let him down. All through the spring. Hero of my own life, who else would it be?

> *Bernice moves gracefully in her own world: the Evangelist and the Dancer observe each other.*

When I grow up I'm going to be—I'm dancing with Baryshnikov. I'm dancing with Nijinsky, even if he's dead and I wish he wasn't, ha! I'm dancing with—my dancer.

> *The men dance formally, a tango, heads averted from each other.*

Evangelist: Board o' Governors meeting last night. We're worried. You've got to find more revenue.

Bernice: Attracted to danger.

Dancer: You've only given me six months. A limited budget.

           Moving towards them, fascinated.

Bernice: Dancer, danger, just one letter different.

Evangelist: Projections said there would be more. By now. You need to be self-generating.

Bernice: I'm dangerous myself, like.

Dancer: It takes time. It is new, and strange.

Bernice: Dance with me.

Evangelist: There's a recession. We don't *have* time.

Bernice: *(To them, following.)* I knew I'd be something, ever since I knew anything.

Evangelist: Go on the air again.

Dancer: Too much money.

Bernice: Singled out for something important.

Evangelist: Spend it to make it.

Dancer: No more to spend.

Bernice: *(Pleading.)* Something—wonderful.

Evangelist: We all have our crosses to bear. Good day.

           The men break apart, disappear their separate ways.

Bernice: It couldn't not come. It couldn't! Dance with me!

           (To audience.) Don't give up! Never let ye suffer nor let ye be afraid. It will come to you too, if ye have faith. I know it. I'm sure of it. I've been in the trough of despond too, you know, many a time. I've been there

and I've felt it. Lots of times. Dave knows, he does. He—
(She covers her mouth.)

> *Dave, cap in hand, appears.*

Dave: *(To the Doctor.)* At the movies, every Saturday—when
           we were courting—she'd have her load of Kleenexes
           stuffed in her pocket and her parents'd say, have a good
           time, Bernice—

Bernice: Toads.

Dave: —mind, Dave, you bring her back now, all the way to
           the door… Well, I always did, don't know why they
           said that. I'd always bring her home. And she'd be
           sitting there in the dark every Saturday by my side. She
           didn't like me reaching for her, said it was wrong—

Bernice: Falling out.

Dave: —so I'd just wait.

Bernice: Put 'em back.

> *(Stuffs them back into her mouth.)*

Dave: —And by and by her hand'd creep over into my lap; I'd
           wait for her to come to me like some little wounded
           thing, fluttering into the warmth. With her other hand
           she'd be blowing her nose and sniffling at the sad parts,
           but I'd have a big smile on. And we'd both enjoy those
           movies, in our own way.

Bernice: There. All gone.

Dave: *(Into her space.)* Want me to wait for you, Bern?

Bernice: No. You go on home.

Dave: Back in an hour?

Bernice: I can find my own way. Go on, now. Go.

> *He goes. The Dancer is rubbing his head with a towel.*

Bernice: I'm here.

Dancer: Right on time, Bernice. As always.

Bernice: Where are the others?

Dancer: I tried to call you, but no answer. I'm closed today. I
          have the flu.

Bernice: Closed?

Dancer: I'm sorry you came all this way.

Bernice: ...No trouble. Is it...?

Dancer: Ah, it's not your problem. But thank you.

Bernice: Anything I can do? I mean it.

Dancer: Thank you, Bernice. Another time, uh?

Bernice: Maybe—

Dancer: I'm sorry.

>   *She backs away.*

Bernice: He needed me, my dancer! I could see it, I could taste it.
          I didn't know what to do, how to get his trust. I went to
          God that Sunday, like I always did. And—at last, at
          last—He sent The Sign!

>   *The Evangelist takes his place at the head of his
>   congregation.*

Evangelist: Hold not thy peace, O God of my praise: For the mouth
          of the wicked and the mouth of the deceitful are opened
          against me. For my love they are my adversaries: but I
          give myself unto prayer.

>   *The congregation, murmuring, speaking in tongues.
>   Bernice turns this way and that, watching them fall to
>   the ground.*

They have rewarded me evil for good, and hatred for my love—

(Continuing, soft, under Bernice's following speech.)—Set thou a wicked man over him: and let Satan stand at his right hand. When he shall be judged, let him be condemned; and let his prayer become sin.

Bernice: And I knew who they were thinking about, I knew who he was referring to. I did, you know. It was their fear of him, that he was different. And I opened my mouth for him, but all that come out was this desperate—

(Solo, she croaks.) Awwk!

Evangelist: *(Solo.)* Let his days be few; and let another take his office!

(Continuing, soft, under Bernice's following speech.) Let his wife and children be continually vagabonds, and beg: let them seek their bread also out of their desolate places. Let there be none to extend mercy unto him: neither let there be any to favour his fatherless children, and in the generation following let their name be blotted out.

Bernice: And I felt so sorry for him, my dancer. I knew that's who they were speaking of, wanting to spoil his labour and all that he had, stop him from dancing and sweating so beautiful, in his desolate places, and wearing those clothes. But they'd got it wrong. He had no wife or widow, he had no children, no one would give him the chance—

(Solo.)—but I would, I wanted to yell out—I would! I would!

Evangelist: *(Continuing, soft, under Bernice's following speech.)* Let the iniquity of his fathers be remembered with the Lord; and let not the sin of his mother be blotted out. Let them be before the Lord continually, that he may cut off the memory of them from the earth. Because that he remembered not to shew mercy, but persecuted the poor and needy man, that he might even slay the broken in heart—

Bernice: —I could feel his hands, those fingertips that flew through the air, that touched the sky. I could feel his hands and fingers running down my body, over my breasts. I could feel them and I was frightened that someone would see, would see him touching me and making me swoon, just swoon there where I stood with his dancer's fingers, his artist's soul coming into my mouth!

The Evangelist's words pour through her.

Evangelist: *(Solo)* —For I am poor and needy, and my heart is wounded within me! My knees are weak through fasting; and my flesh faileth of fatness!

Bernice cries out in real ecstasy and falls to the ground, her hands between her legs.

(In the reverberating silence.) I will greatly praise the Lord with my mouth; yea, I will praise him among the multitude.

He exits. She lies there, under the statue.

Bernice: …After that, I just felt so peaceful, you know, so good in myself, I knew I was loved, I just knew it. He wasn't where I'd been looking for him, not in the church, you know. He was never there. He was in the dark and the warm with the smell of the earth, the smell of our blood, pumping. In the dark. We had to keep it quiet or they'd get mad at us. They'd send him away and so I was very circumspect. I was oh, so careful.

She rolls onto her side.

I'd be lying there beside that man, that man in the trailer, but in the night, oh, in the night *he'd* send his dog—he had this huge dog with these enormous eyes that spun like a millwheel and was his servant— and he'd send this dog for me, and I was light and that and I'd climb upon the dog's back, and he would carry me to him, to my dancer, to his bed, and we'd make love all night long there in his room. And he was so tender with me. He touched me in my secret places and he knew what I liked and he was never in a hurry. Never, never. And we'd be there for hours, never just fast and hard, always slow and smooth and beautiful. And I'd lick his sweat and he'd lick my—

—What was I saying?

The Dancer puts on his shirt. She sits up, fixes on him.

Uh. Well, in the classes we'd be so careful, eh, with all these other women there. He'd never look me in the eye, you know, and I wouldn't look at him. Like, he started even to go overboard, you know, avoiding looking at me and sometimes he'd spend time chatting with one of the others and it'd—it'd just, like, kill me, but I knew he was doing it for show. But it'd just, like, *kill* me.

The Dancer tucks his shirt into his pants.

Kill me. It would.

He sees her eyeing him. She looks away.

And my middle one was wanting me to read to her, and so I did, you know. I want my kids to grow up smart and well-read. It's important in this world. And we just happened to be reading the story of *The Magic Tinderbox.* You know that one? A soldier climbs down inside a tree and finds this magic box for the old witch he met on the road—he comes out of the tree and cuts off the witch's head because she's old and ugly, and he finds out the box will make him rich and grant him wishes. And he has dogs for servants!—sound familiar? With millwheel eyes, that's right! Well *that's* funny, I thought. And I kept on reading. And he wishes for the princess, and the dog brings her to him and—well, you know, I remembered reading that story when I was a child. And then dreaming of it now. And I thought, that's prophetic. That's one of those prophetic things that tell you what to do next. It was, you know. He was waiting for me.

I'm here for my class.

Dancer: No classes today, Bernice. Remember? Thursday I dance. Work on my own work, yes?

Bernice: Can I watch you?

Dancer: Well...

Bernice: I won't be any trouble.

Dancer: I... this piece is brand new, just forming in my mind. Many false starts, wrong steps—

Bernice: I won't mind.

Dancer: But sometime, if there's someone watching, Bernice, the mind seizes up, yes? It worries about the watcher, not the creation. You see?

Bernice: You don't want me.

Dancer: No, no, don't say that. I welcome my students to see my work. I stumble, too. I tell you that. But this one—it's so new. You have children, yes? Like—that first moment with a newborn. Very private. Very intimate. So soft, so close. Too personal.

Bernice: Oh, yes... Please. Let me stay.

Dancer: I... I don't know how to say this, Bernice, but...I have a lot on my mind.

Bernice: But...

Dancer: *(Frustrated.)* I need not to be looked at every moment, you know?

The spell is broken. Bernice stumbles away.

Bernice: He said that, to me. To *me*, who all along was watching out for him, protecting him, writing him cheques, cheques! to keep him going, from the baby bonus, and he…said that to me. He's an artist. He's on the air! He's out there, flying—he has no right to say that. To me. To say it! No right.

So I kept quiet, but I kept thinking, and these ideas kept exploding round in my head. I had to make something happen! It had to come. And in that story, in *The Tinderbox*, the princess was so innocent. She didn't mean to cause such a stir, she never meant… She never did… She said, while they were drinking tea in the throne room, she said—

Dave enters, with a bag full of groceries.

I had this strange dream last night, about a dog and a— a man. The dog came into the room, and I was made to get up on its back, and it took me to this man's room— and the man—kissed me.

Dave: That *is* a strange dream, Bernie. A dog, eh? Maybe I should shave more. Ha.

Bernice: Don't be filthy.

Dave: Oh, now. I hoped maybe you'd laugh, Bern. Have a laugh at me, eh, like we used to. Huh?

Bernice: That's not funny.

Dave: I thought it was.

Bernice: That's not funny. Not funny.

Dave: Ok, Bern. Ok. Poor joke. I got the peanut butter you wanted.

Bernice: Don't care.

Dave: And the chips.

Bernice: I don't eat chips. You know that.

Dave: Well, someone does. And you know it's not me.

Bernice: I don't know anything. You can do what you please.

Dave: Oh, Bern. What does it matter who eats the chips? Huh? C'mon. Be my old Bern.

Bernice: I'm not your old Bern! I'm not! Who the hell are you to be calling me that? If you only knew—if you knew, you'd—

Dave: I'd what? C'mon, get it off your chest. Whatever it is. Your deep dark secret. Huh, Bern? I can take it. Sweetheart.

Bernice: Get out from underfoot! Get out! Tracking up my kitchen again. It's enough to—honest to God.

Dave: Sometimes, Bernie. Sometimes, you gotta wonder.

He goes.

Bernice: *(Calls after him.)* Don't you want to hear about the man? No. 'Course not!

Becoming progressively more agitated.

It's hard, it is! Too hard. The which is which, the toads, I can't keep nothing down. I warned him, I tried to say— but oh, no, Bernice, no, no. Well, so then. Well, we'll just see what we shall see!

And God said Be fruitful, and multiply, and replenish the earth, and *subdue* it. Make it do what it should. Make it over. Make it *right. Make* it right!

The Dancer warms up. She doesn't look at him, but is aware of him, his body. She takes a big bottle of Coke from the grocery bag, takes a long swallow.

Thirsty. Always. Thirsty. The dust, so dusty out here, all summer long. And the sweat. Sweat makes you thirsty.

I look around me. It's not right. It's not right for one to have so much and the other to have nothing. To have— all that, all that flight, all that grace, all that beauty, all that *life!* And the other. To have nothing. What does it avail ye, that body, those gifts of speed and joy—what useful purpose does that beauty serve if ye thereby just forsake the world, forsake the others, ignore them? Unaware, of all that...hunger. Unafraid. It's not right. It's not necessary.

Like the magpie, my magpie on the farm—he never heard me. He never paid attention. He was too busy, too occupied with his own concerns and serve him right. Serve him so *right*. Serve him *right!* Why did God grant him such a beautiful tail, when a short, stubby one would do? Why! Why?

The Evangelist appears as the Dancer disappears.

Evangelist: What can I do for you, Bernice?

Bernice: Well, I'm troubled. I have to tell you that. I'm troubled. I want to do right.

Evangelist: Of course you do. How can I help you do right?

Bernice: It's this dream. I didn't know who else to come to, who else would know what I should do, Father.

Evangelist: Not "Father," Bernice. I've told you. But you can confide in me, if you need my guidance. You know that, after all this time.

Bernice: I need it, I know it, I need it! *(A litany:)* In this dream. I have it often, this dream. I'm carried away, against my will. I don't will it. It just happens. He brings me to him. I'm on the dog's back. I'm carried to him. To his room. To his bed.

Evangelist: Whose bed? What are you talking about?

Bernice: I'm so ashamed. I've kept it secret for so long. *(She darts a glance at him.)* It's not just a dream. It's true. It's true, so help me God.

Evangelist: All right, Bernice, it's true. Tell me what you've done.

Bernice: I've been away from Dave, from my husband? I've been away from his bed on many nights. My dancing class nights. That's how it started. He's a good man, Dave. He hasn't called the police, but he is afraid. I'm the only one who knows where I go. You can check with him, with Dave, he'll tell you it's true, that I stay away at nights—it's true!

Evangelist: All right, Bernice, all right. Do you want to tell me where you go? Is that why you came to me?

Bernice: I don't want to, no, but I have to. I have to! It's the dancer. He calls me to him, and I can't say no. I can't say no to him. We do it every chance we get. We do it in his bed and on his couch and in front of the mirrors on the floor. We do it all the time, all the time, and I stay with him all night. I stay out all night with him. And I've told Cheryl my friend, and I told my neighbour and everyone knows. Everyone knows but Dave and my children. They don't know, but everyone knows—I've told them all!

> *She is panting.*

Evangelist: I knew it would come to this. The smug bastard. Do you know what you are telling me?

Bernice: I know, I know, I know.

Evangelist: And do you want me to deal with this?

Bernice: Yes! Take this cup away from me, take it, make it over, make it right!

> *The Evangelist enters the Dancer's studio.*

(A frightened whimper.) Come back…

During the following, Bernice crawls to the Dancer, holds onto his thigh. The men are not aware of her presence.

Evangelist: —and is it true?

Dancer: …Bernice Marshall? Which one is she?

Evangelist: Big woman. Not much of a looker.

Dancer: That isn't kind. Or helpful.

Evangelist: We get your sort here in our town, and this is what happens.

Dancer: Excuse me, but you step out of line. Now. The story again—

Evangelist: She comes to me for help. Accuses you. She is frightened—

Dancer: She is bored!

Evangelist: You don't even know which one—

Dancer: I know. I know now. Bernice. Yes. She is bored. I am kind to her. I try to be. Nothing more.

Evangelist: Then where does she go, all night? A fat woman, out in the dark by herself. No, she goes somewhere.

Dancer: How should I know? Hot summer nights, forever sunsets—she gets in a field and just walks. Walks off. Why should she come back? Straight on to wherever.

Evangelist: Better than one of our little girls, that's all I can say. Corrupting a middle-aged woman who should know better is one thing, but the moment you touch—

Dancer: Now, this is too much. How dare you?

Evangelist: Keep your hands off our daughters or—

Dancer: Damn your white-bread hypocrisy and your corn silk daughters! Bring her here! Make her say it to my face! She's making it all up. Bring her here and see!

Bernice: Nooooo!

She is between them, this is reality; she will rarely meet the eyes of either of the men.

Evangelist: All right, Bernice. Do you want to tell me again what you told me before?

Bernice: *(Small voice.)* No.

Evangelist: And why not?

Bernice: I can't.

Evangelist: Why can't you?

Bernice: He's here.

Evangelist: I know he's here. That is the purpose of our meeting. To uncover the truth.

Bernice: I can't.

Evangelist: He already knows. Everything you told me. But we must hear it from you.

Bernice: No.

Evangelist: We must, for you to have peace. For us to move on, hm?

Bernice: No!

Dancer: Wait, perhaps I'd—

Evangelist: I understand my congregation's needs. Now please don't interfere. Bernice. You are here voluntarily, aren't you?

She nods.

You came to me for help, didn't you?

Again, a small nod.

Why won't you tell me what you told me?

Bernice: Because.

Evangelist: Because why?

Bernice: It's not…

Evangelist: Not what?

Bernice: He wouldn't like me to—

Evangelist: No, Bernice!

Dancer: Really, I—

Evangelist: Please! *(To her.)* Why won't you tell us?

Bernice: I…

Evangelist: *Say* it, Bernice. Say what it is that prevents you from telling me what you told me before.

Bernice: Because it's not…

Evangelist: Not *what?*

Bernice: I can't!

Evangelist: *Say* it! It's not *what?*

        He bangs his hand down, and Bernice cowers.

        I see. Now I see. I should have known. So where *do* you go, Bernice? When you are away from your husband?

Bernice: I can't…

Evangelist: Where do you go?

Bernice: I told you. It was a secret. I never meant—

Evangelist: Ah! You never meant me to take you seriously? You are lying about this too. Where did you go!

Bernice: The park.

Evangelist: Where!

Bernice: The park! Under the statue, there's a place I go.

Evangelist: Under the statue.

Bernice: It's dark and warm.

Evangelist: Why do you go there?

Bernice: It doesn't matter.

Evangelist: It does. Why do you go there?

Bernice: Not just there. I go other places!

Evangelist: Other places. Now we have it! Other places. By *yourself.* To hide away. To worry your husband. To hurt him. To puff yourself up, Bernice, to make yourself important.

Bernice: No! Not true!

Evangelist: It's what?

Bernice: It's not true!

Evangelist: Exactly! It's not true. All the things you've been telling me are not true. And if your story is not true, then what is it?

Bernice: Stop it!

Evangelist: It's all in your head, and it's not true. And what does that make it? This rumour you've been spreading?

Bernice: Not a rumour!

Evangelist: Yes.

Bernice: A dream!

Evangelist: A dream. A fiction. A lie!

Bernice: *(Covering her ears.)* No!

Evangelist: Look at me. It never happened.

Bernice: It—

Evangelist: Say it, Bernice. "It never happened. I made it all up out of my head. It's not real." Say it.

Bernice: It's not—*(She stops.)*

Evangelist: Say it, Bernice.

Bernice: It's not...real. *(She begins to sob.)*

Evangelist: Say it after me: It never happened.

Bernice: *(Sobbing openly.)* It—never happened.

Evangelist: I made it up out of my head.

Bernice: I made it—up—out of my head.

Evangelist: It's not real.

Bernice: It's—not real. Not. Real.

> *Her grief is real and rending. She is confronting a death.*
>
> *Pause.*

Dancer: *(Soft.)* Oh, god.

Evangelist: Good. That's good, Bernice. You've been under a lot of tension. You have stress at home, don't you?

> *Bernice nods, still sobbing.*

There's not enough money, too many mouths to feed. Isn't that right? You have needs, don't you, Bernice? You have aspirations. You have a hard row to hoe.

Now. Bernice. You must apologize to this artist. He is a guest in our town. We are lucky to have him.

He shoots the Dancer a look of open dislike.

Bernice: I—I'm sorry. I'm sorry. I apologize.

Pause.

Dancer: May I say something?

Evangelist: It would be better—

Dancer: Tell the Board. I am leaving here, I will be leaving, I will not stay, I cannot. I won't. But I've learned much. You may *want* it, the dance, the life of the mind, the life of the spirit and the body. You may *want* it. But there must be room. Yes?

Evangelist: I *don't* want it.

Dancer: I know.

Pause.

I am sorry, Bernice. I am sorry that this happened. This cruelty. I am sorry, for you.

He goes.

Evangelist: All right, Bernice? We'll fix you up. All right?

He goes. She is alone.

Bernice: …*I* want it. I've always wanted it. And I've never had it.

Come back…

Dave appears.

Dave: (*To the Doctor.*) I knew where she was. The park at the end of our street. Knew she was safe in there, out of the wind. No one would bother her. She could think. I kept an eye on her. Wasn't none of his business, way I see it.

Coming between a man and his wife, thinking he's the saviour. Should have kept his big nose out of it.

> *Bernice sniffs. She takes a drink of Coke, wipes her nose. She sees chips in the grocery bag, begins to eat mechanically.*

Bernice: *(Very soft.)* Mine eyes have seen the glory
>   of the coming of the Lord,
> He is trampling on the vintage
>   where the grapes of wrath are stored,
> He is something something something
>   with his terrible swift sword
> His truth is marching on.

Don't look at me like that. I don't want you looking, doing the playback. Stupid woman's shame. Conflict pure and simple, eh? Not so bloody simple. Huh.

Under the statue. In the park. A musty funk, some furry animal or little boys going pee pee in the dirt. All worked in. All warm. My statue above me, tons of metal, heavy, heavy above me. Some fella going off to battle, or coming back from battle, sparks flying round his eyes at the smell of blood and death. The glory. First and Second World Wars. Fighting the big ones, not the small and stupid. Making it worthwhile. All our young men on the plaques he'd be, dead for their country. Double, triple lists. Name after name after name.

It's warm and dark lying here, underneath him. Lying here, loving that. All that weight.

> *She sniffs, an exciting idea begins to grow.*

I want to *be* him. I do. Be that angry, be that righteous, do the glory, for *myself*, for once. Thrust! Into the wind. Into the air. Getting off the ground!

> *She drinks.*

My Ma'd kill me. Hear me say that. You get your hands away from yourself, you filthy girl. Like a toad you are, you slimy thing. Never knew me, don't know her. Nor my dad, nor my brothers. Red faces, too much drinking, too much yelling. Huh...

I haven't a clue what goes on in the heads of my kids. And I'll tell you something else for nothing—I don't want to.

It's too much.

Dave: *(To the Doctor.)* I brought a blanket for her legs, for the drive back. She feels the cold, so I remembered the blanket—it's the one she likes, the one she used for nursing. She's a good mother, she surely is. When Cheryl come to me, told me what Bernie was saying 'bout that feller—well I was hurt. I'll say that. I was...

Well. I want to see her now. She's had enough of being away. I've had enough of her mother. Time we got going, back 'fore dark, 'fore the kids have supper. She'll come around, I know she will, soon's she sees them. They've always brought her round. Me, I'm not so... Well. The hand doesn't steal over into the warmth and dark no more. I have to go fetch it.

He disappears. Bernice, alone, is quite still, inert.

Doctor: *(Off.)* Bernice? You coming along now?

Bernice: Huh?

Doctor: The kids are waiting. And your mother.

Bernice: No.

The Doctor enters.

Doctor: You're all packed, I see. You're ready.

Bernice: No!

Doctor: Believe me, Bernice. You're ready to go.

Bernice: Five minutes. Just give me—give me time?

He looks at her carefully, then smiles.

Doctor: A little gift. Between you and me. Ok?

He goes. She eats another mouthful of chips, thoughtful.

Bernice: No. Uh uh. Oh, no, Bernice, no no… There. You got time. To lie on your bed. Talk to the other women. All the time in the world. Talk civilized. Talk gentle, do watercolours.

She laughs, rocks; agitated.

Steady on, Bernice. You're getting silly, girl. You just be an example to your brothers. You just get some sense, girl. Stay out of the muck. You don't need to go in there. You're a big girl now. Such a big girl. Hey, you're a little butterball, Bernie, aren't you? Hey, just a growing thing. You're a fat girl, Bernice, yes you are. You're a big fat woman!

Nooo!

She flings the chips in an arc around her head. She twists the chip bag into a brand, menacing.

No, you can't stop fate, no matter who you are—nor that truck that's coming along the highway, nor that hawk that swoops down from the sky and carries you away in the blink of an eye with his claws in your guts: "I'm not ready!" You can't stop it. Even your beauty's no defense. Against what you got coming to you. Even your grace.

I got close to one once, a magpie. I started telling you. He was yanking and yanking on this worm in the ground. Looked like he hadn't had a square meal in days, he was that engrossed. It was when I was a kid, out tramping around on the farm. No, that must be wrong, because I had a pair of scissors and—

She freezes, as Dave clears his throat outside.

I will, goddammit! Puke out the toads, I'm gonna puke them out. So shut up. Shut. Up.

Ok. Ok, I see him. There he is, my magpie, the one that lives in the pine trees down by the mail box, the one I think about all the time, all winter long, the one my dad cuffed me for. 'Cause he didn't know the answer as to why he had that gorgeous tail. *(A cry.)* The magpie's tail...!

Dave: Bern? You ok in there?

Bernice: *(Speeding up.)* So he's tugging away at this worm, eh, and I put my books down, real quiet, and he keeps tugging. I sneak up; he never hears me, he's so happy—

No, I—*(Struggling with herself.)*—uh—

Ok, I put my hand in my pocket. It's spring. I remember I have on my spring coat with the big pockets, and I keep sneaking up and he never hears me and then I—

The Dancer appears, in counterpoint.

Dave: Bernie?

Bernice: *(Becoming more agitated.)*—I step on his tail! And he goes berserk, eh? He starts trying to twist around and peck my rubber boots, and his legs are jumping up and down, and he starts croaking. Oh, God help me. He can't figure it out, he can't, forgets all about that juicy worm, and I just look at him. I just look at him and up close, you know, I think—up close, he's not that good-looking. Up close, he's just noisy and smelly and stupid—a bird brain's tiny, so he's bound to be stupid, right? Up close.

Dave: Something going on in there?

Bernice: I want to see what will happen. So I put my hand in my pocket, and I pull on my gloves. I have these nice red gloves, and I take out this pair of scissors. I'm working on a home ec project, that's right, and I took the scissors home to trim my hair 'cause we don't have any that sharp—they're *real* sharp—and I reach down. I'm just curious, eh? And he's going so crazy, I think, you stupid bird, so I just—

Dave: Doctor, I think you'd—

Bernice: —*(Sobbing.)* Let me tell it. Let me stay inside and see it. Let me tell my fucking life!

   Everything but Bernice disappears.

I cut his tail off!

   (She's going to be sick.)

It's too much. There's too much of him. It isn't fair. I tell him he's vain and gaudy and should learn to live without it. That's what my dad tells *me*, he says don't be stupid, what do you want to be reading that junk about movie stars and preema donnas for? You're getting above yourself. And that's what I tell *him*. The bird. And I watch him hop away. He still can hop. His tail isn't necessary, you know. I found that out.

   Panting, mouth open.

I hide in the ditch when the bus comes by for me, and after it goes on, I come out and I watch that magpie for hours. Watch everything that happens. Watch it panting with its mouth open. Watch his cockiness melt away. Watch the changes, what it'd done to him.

He was different, see? He wasn't beautiful anymore. He was just another bird. He was heavy and clumsy and he had to work real hard to get off the ground.

But he did it. Eventually.

He flew away.

   She takes matches from her pocket.

And so I wondered. I wondered why God had given him those feathers after all. If he could still fly. Didn't seem fair… He could still fly away.

She sets the chip bag alight. In memory: Dave enters, rumpled from sleep.

Dave: Bernie? What the hell are you doing? Bern?

Bernice: Just never you mind. Never mind.

She is trying to set the trailer on fire.

Dave: Hold it, Bernice! For Christ's sake, woman, what's got into you!

Bernice: Let me go. Let me—

Dave: Shit, I—

She turns the brand on herself.

Bernie! Hold it! Good Christ, we're—

He wrestles her to the ground. Holds her until she is still. She lies, inert.

Now stay there, woman. We need some help. Just stay where you are.

He exits.

Pause.

Bernice: You thinking I kept that tail? Kept it as a souvenir? Well, you'd be wrong. I cut it up in little pieces and put it in the ground.

Silence, dark. The Dancer enters, cautious.

Doctor: (*Voice.*) Bernice. We're ready for you.

She sits up. Sees the Dancer. Turns away. He moves closer. She moves away. He moves closer, tries a little strut. She scrambles to her feet, watches him. He grows bolder. He moves, dances, hops, then struts boldly. She laughs, claps her hands. He takes fright, dances away.

She approaches the audience.

Bernice: Now this is why I come to you. The multitudes. I just about forgot. I want to save you, keep you from the pain and the heartache I bin through. Listen.

Doctor: Bernice.

Bernice: I got to hurry. This is it. If you have life and energy in you, they want it. They want it so much. They'll do anything. They'll rip it out of you. Keep it for themselves. That's where I went wrong, trying to make them see. But this is what I've figgered: what they say's not necessary, what they say is filthy's the only thing worth having. So I'm a toad, so what? It's still there, all my own, my diamond in the dark. Sharp and shining. In the belly.

I'm gonna keep it hid.

The Dancer hops, struts. She gives a tiny hop back.

Doctor: *(Enters.)* You must be packed by now. You're just procrastinating.

Bernice: You're right, I am. *(She laughs.)* I am! But I'm not ready to go back.

Doctor: Sure you are. It doesn't mean I won't see you anymore, Bernice.

Bernice: Tell Dave I've got to rest, eh? I've got this eating—

Doctor: Yes, that's all taken care of. He'll help you. He will. Let's go, hm?

Bernice: …When'd you say you'd be seeing me?

Doctor: Remember? We've talked about this a lot. You'll be coming here twice a week. We'll see each other then.

Bernice: You promise me?

Doctor: That's the normal course of treatment. I see everyone twice a week if they can manage it.

Bernice: Think that's enough? What if I need to come more often?

Doctor: We'll cross that bridge when we get to it.

Bernice: Good.

Doctor: You'll be fine. I give you my word of honour, hm?

Bernice smiles a secret smile.

Doctor: What's so funny?

Bernice: Never mind. Twice a week?

He nods, holds out his hand to her. She takes his hand, they begin to move off; the Doctor exits.

The Dancer erupts into a final dance, using all the space. Bernice has turned back—she opens her arms, and he leaps into the air. She is one with him for that one moment: free, open, flying.

END

HAVING

For Gordon McCall,
and for Andrew Willmer, with love and thanks.
And Punch, who came back.

"We must choose with great caution the folk heroes we present to one another and the qualities they embody, for they shall surely return to haunt us."
—Elliott Leyton, anthropologist

"...in the absence of a vision there are nightmares"
—Bruce Cockburn

Production Credits

Having was first produced at the Centaur Theatre in Montreal, Quebec, in 1999.

Directed by Rona Waddington
Set and Costume design by Guido Tondino
Lighting Design by Robert Krause
Original Music by David Sereda
Dramaturged by Gordon McCall
Stage Managed by Chris Hidalgo, and A.S.M. Kieran Keller

CAST
Carolyn Hetherington as Olivia
Helen King as Erin
Stephanie McNamara as Manon
Hugh Thompson as Jemmy
John Robinson as David

Great thanks to Gord McCall for his leap of faith, his passion for Canadian theatre, and the insightful dramaturgical journey we took together. To Andrew, always. To the strong and dedicated cast, to Rona, Guido, and Robbo, and the incredible Centaur team. Also Jeremy Bouchard, Julia Dover, Maureen Epp, David King, Marjorie Malpass, Robert Ross Parker and Laura Teasdale, for a wonderful initial workshop on themes from *Moll Flanders*, to Concordia University and friends and colleagues there who have assisted me in many ways, to Bruce Willmer of Hemmera Resource Consultants for technical advice on waste management (any mistakes are my own!). And to many generous others, thanks.

Dramaturg's Notes

Capturing a story idea is similar to catching a butterfly on the wing with your bare hands. It has to be caught with lightning dexterity and held with gentleness so as not to crush the life out of it. Once it is captured, the real work begins…taking a story idea and turning it into a play, surely one of the most difficult forms of writing one can undertake.

Kit Brennan brought me not one, but three story ideas in the fall of 1997. We chose one together and after almost two years, three readings and nine drafts, this brand new play *Having* took the final step in its creation. It went "from page to stage."

From the first day of rehearsal to opening night, the infusion of life, chemistry, imagination, talent, expectation, anxiety, dedication to the intent of the play, and faith in Kit and her dramatic vision provided by the artistic and production team combined to provide an exhilarating meeting with the audience in the most wonderful moment of all: the realization of a dream and the birth of a new play.

It was a true pleasure to share the creative journey with Kit. She is a writer with a dramatic vision that excites me. Her theatrical imagination is vivid and daring. She provokes an audience to view events in a manner that may not have occurred to them but which they ultimately feel could be viewed in no other way. She writes with extensive knowledge of her subject matter but with the freedom that her imagination excites. She builds layer by layer through each draft until each character's journey is not only complete, but meshed seamlessly with its fellow travellers'. She has that rare ability to capture a fleeting story idea and turn it into a play.

—Gordon McCall

Director's Notes

In today's society, we are less and less defined by what we are, and more and more by what we have. A good salary, a bad job, three children, two cars, cancer, epilepsy... However enormous or trivial, these are the criteria by which we are measured, by which we measure ourselves. Having has become a yardstick for personal assessment. It has replaced doing, dreaming, even happiness. In many ways, *having* has replaced *being*.

As a director, nothing compares to the excitement of working on a new script. As an audience member, I cherish a premiere as a unique experience, an evening of risk and discovery...the moment when the artistic team and the spectator are at their closest, both driven by faith, curiosity and genuine human interest.

In *Having*, Kit has explored and brought together two worlds, each with its own set of contradictions: contemporary North America, with its duality of technological progress and yearning for a return to more "human" values; and the ethereal, lyrical world of the 18th century highwayman, with its intense romanticism and dark reality.

—Rona Waddington

Staging Notes

CHARACTERS

David Dafoe: 45 years old, a waste management consultant

Erin Dafoe: 17 years old, David's daughter

Manon Tremblay: 38 years old, David's new employee, an environmental engineer

Olivia Dafoe: 70 years old, David's mother

Jemmy Ferguson: same age as David, an 18th century highwayman (Captain Thunderball)

SETTING

The action takes place in David's house in the city (living room/office, Erin's bedroom), and in Olivia's house in the country (living room).

Notes

"The Highwayman" by Alfred Noyes is used with the permission of John Murray (Publishers) Ltd. For production, permission to use the extracts from the poem as indicated in this script must be obtained from John Murray (Publishers) Ltd., 50 Albemarle St., London UK, W1X 4BD.

The play should flow, with crossfades rather than blackouts, except where a blackout is making a definite end. The music should have a rhythm like galloping hooves, which grows in intensity as the play goes on.

When Jemmy appears to Erin, he is real and very physical—right in her room with her, larger than life. When he appears to Olivia, he is less so, more in her senses, in her imagination. At the end of the play, David senses Jemmy's real presence for the very first time. In the first production, this differentiation was accomplished through the use of a scrim. The bedroom, which was raised, was fully scrimmed and also became Jemmy's lookout, from Scene 8 on.

Act One

> *Olivia is sitting by a window. She is recalling a poem,*
> *trying to remember.*

Olivia: "The wind was a torrent of darkness
      among the gusty trees,
  The moon was a ghostly galleon
      tossed upon cloudy seas,
  The road was a ribbon of moonlight
      over the purple moor—"

> *Joining in with and taking over from Olivia, a young*
> *woman's voice sings the verse, sounding like Olivia, but*
> *younger and carefree. Underscoring is a rhythm of*
> *galloping hoofbeats, coming closer. Olivia, by the end, is*
> *in pain, trying to breathe through it.*

Voice: "—road was a ribbon of moonlight
      over the purple moor—
  And the highwayman came riding —
    Riding, riding—
  The highwayman came riding, up to the old inn-door."

> *During the verse, elsewhere on the stage, a moon fills the*
> *sky—and a horse neighs. A man, tightly lit, dressed in a*
> *worn velvet frock coat, lace at the cuffs, high boots, and*
> *a hat with a cocked feather, is looking intently into the*
> *night, towards the audience. We see just enough to*
> *register this image, and then he disappears,*
> *simultaneously with lights out on Olivia and up on*
> *Erin's bedroom.*

> *Erin is sitting in front of her computer. She blinks at what she has just "seen." David enters, sees her.*

David: Erin? You ok?

Erin: …Yeah.

David: What's going on?

Erin: I'm fine, it's ok.

David: So what do you think of the changes? It's temporary, but—

Erin: It's kind of—weird, Dad. Walking in and there's all your work stuff.

David: Top of the line. New computers. Even newer than yours. You should be jealous.

Erin: Yeah, but I know how to use mine.

> *His cellphone rings. Erin rolls her eyes.*

David: *(Into phone.)* Yeah? Yeah, the airport. I'm going there tomorrow, check it out.

> *Erin goes back to her computer.*

No, piece of cake. They like us, Steve, don't panic. Right. Later. *(He hangs up.)*

Erin: Is Steve there already?

David: The new office opens in a month.

Erin: You're the only one left?

David: Manon's stayed back—she's helping with the environmental components on the airport transaction. Steve's got the rest of the team with him in Calgary.

Erin: You didn't say there'd be someone else—working in the house.

David: I can't keep it going alone. There's too much happening, couple of big prospectives.

     Erin looks at him.

Erin: She'll be here too? In the living room?

David: The office. It's only temporary.

Erin: *(Beat.)* ...You stayed 'cause of me, didn't you, Dad?

David: Well, yeah, your last year—you've got to get the scholarships, keep your old man out of the poor house. Ah, it's gonna be great, Erin. I don't have to wear a suit.

     Erin smiles.

    I'd like Manon to come tonight, that ok?

Erin: I thought it was just Nan coming.

David: I got mousse cake, basil chicken, all your favourites. Got to celebrate that driver's license. It's a major event!

Erin: Why'd you invite someone else if it's my license we're celebrating?

David: I thought it'd be fun!

Erin: You should have told me.

David: Well, I'm *asking* you.

Erin: You'll talk about work all night.

David: I won't! Well, just a little—I promise. Anyway, Mum loves hearing about Geoterme. It helps her feel part of things. *(Looking at the screen.)* Hey, "hazardous waste cleanup." Look at that.

     He reaches over and scrolls down, engrossed. She looks at him, then away.

Erin: Dad? You got into waste management because you
           wanted to change things, right? Make a difference?

David: Yeah, yeah, growth industry.

           David checks his watch.

           So can I call her, say it's ok?

Erin: *(Shrugs.)* Sure.

           *He leaves. Erin closes her eyes; she has a pounding
           headache. Sound of galloping rises suddenly, a horse's
           labouring breath, coming closer quickly. Erin looks up,
           disoriented. Blackout.*

Scene 2

           *Later that night, after dinner. David's living room,
           furnished with upscale office furniture and equipment
           Olivia, Manon and David enter.*

Olivia: —it was marvellous. And that ocean! You must come,
           David. I've been telling you for years.

David: You go on these trips at peak times for me, Mum. I can't
           get away. As I keep telling *you*.

Manon: You didn't go swimming? In Greece?

Olivia: Beaches are for the young, svelte, and unscarred. Though
           I'm in remission, so they tell me.

Manon: Oh, I'm sorry, I—

Olivia: No, no. I'm hoping he'll overlook me—the dark stranger.
           So I don't press my luck.

           Erin enters from the kitchen.

David: Anyone for scotch? Or keep going on the wine?

Manon: Scotch, please.

Olivia: Oh, yes!

> *David puts the wine down, makes the rounds.*

David: You're driving, Mum.

Olivia: And you're an old nursemaid. This is a celebration!

David: Right! There's wine on the sideboard, Erin. Help yourself.

> *Erin does. Olivia, concerned, watches Erin pour a very large glass for herself.*

First and foremost—to Erin's license! Hard won, well deserved. Freedom for her—and for me. Plus. A huge thank you to Manon for staying through the transition. Who knows? Maybe we'll need to keep a branch office here, and maybe you'll be running it. So. To Erin—and Manon.

Manon: Cheers. Thanks.

> *They all toast.*

Olivia: Must you sound so—aggressive all the time, David? That's what *I* consider a major pollutant—everybody out to get more, be bigger, be meaner.

Manon: It's the New World, Mrs. Dafoe.

Olivia: If you read good literature, you see it's not so new. Humans behave this way when they smell disaster. There's something—twisted about what's happening.

Erin: Yeah, like we're destroying the earth we live on and you're making money from it.

David: Hey! Erin, we're the guys cleaning it up!

Olivia: Well, then, it's ethically questionable for you to be so— happy about it!

> *Manon and David look at each other. They try not to smile.*

And why have you turned your lovely living room into this monstrous—showroom?

David: We've got to have somewhere to bring the clients.

Olivia: But where are you going to go to relax?

            David's cellphone rings.

David: We're saving overhead. It's only temporary. *(Into phone.)* Yeah?

Olivia: Such a terrible, competitive life you're all leading.

David: *(Into phone.)* No, the Yellowknife file. You'll find it there.

Manon: In this business, unfortunately, it's the way it's done.

David: *(Into phone.)* Keep looking. Let me know if you—yeah. *(Hangs up.)*

Olivia: I'm not convinced.

Manon: I hear you're keen on technology, Erin. Computers and stuff?

Erin: Not really.

Olivia: *(To Erin.)* Don't tell me you don't read anymore? You were such a romantic little girl! Men in masks and lace— that ballad, do you remember? You were mad for it!

David: Not that thing. "The wind was a something something—"

Olivia: That's right, I read it to you too, didn't I?

David: Ad nauseum. "—and the highwayman came riding, riding, riding. The highwayman came riding—"

            Manon laughs.

What, you know it?

Manon: No.

David: Repeat something often enough and it can't be forgotten—just like advertising.

Olivia: It's poetry, it's the rhythm—the writer did it on purpose, David.

David: Romantic bilge.

Olivia: I loved it!

> *As Olivia speaks, Erin begins to phase out, as in having an aura prior to a seizure.*

I was remembering it so clearly—was that just today? *(To Manon.)* An inn-keeper's daughter has a secret lover, a highwayman. He promises to take her away with him. He's disapproved of, because he's dangerous, and he's free.

Manon: Stand and deliver, that sort of thing?

Olivia: Yes! One night, militiamen break into her room and tie her to her bedpost, with a musket beneath her breast so she won't cry out a warning—for they know he's coming. They're waiting for the sound of his horse, galloping towards them.

Manon: So they can kill him?

Olivia: When the sound of hooves rings out on the road, she pulls the trigger on herself—"she warned him with her death": he hears the shot, and rides off, back into the night.

> *Lights flash for a second on the man. He again is listening intently; as he looks towards them, Erin blinks, comes to, and he disappears. David looks hard at Erin.*

Manon: Doesn't sound like a very fun time for the woman. What happens to *him*? The highwayman?

Olivia: I don't remember that part. But he's gorgeous, I do recall,
            a perfect—gentleman.

            *She recites, with passion. Manon smiles at David, raises
            her eyebrows at him.*

            "He'd a French cocked-hat on his forehead,
                a bunch of lace at his chin,
            A coat of the claret velvet,
                and breeches of brown doeskin:
            They fitted with never a wrinkle;
            his boots were up to the thigh!
            And he rode with a jewelled twinkle,
            His pistol butts a-twinkle,
            His rapier hilt a-twinkle, under the jewelled sky."

David: Very nice, Mum.

Olivia: Oh, you. You were such a solemn little boy, so terrified of
            your own imagination.

David: All that riding, he must at least have stayed in shape.
            How do *you* do it, Manon?

Manon: Swimming. Running. Though it's getting harder.

Olivia: *(Rising.)* On that note, I think *I'll* crawl home to bed. You
            people are far too over-achieving for me. And you know,
            work has *always* been hard, much as your generation
            likes to think you invented it.

Manon: Mrs. Dafoe, it's been a pleasure meeting you.

Olivia: Olivia, please.

Manon: Olivia. 'Night.

            Olivia, David and Erin go to the door.

Olivia: *(To Erin.)* You all right, dear?

Erin: Sure.

Olivia: You know, if you'd ever like—someone else to talk to? I'm always home. Now that you drive, perhaps you could visit? The lake is beautiful in the summers.

David: *(Kissing Olivia's cheek.)* You're looking great, by the way.

Olivia: Think so?

David: Beautiful as ever.

Olivia: Good night, dears.

            She exits.

David: *(Calls.)* Sure you're okay to drive?

Olivia: *(Off.)* You'd think you were *my* parent!

            Erin sees a sweater Olivia's left behind.

Erin: Nan, wait!

            Erin runs out after Olivia. David goes back to Manon.

Manon: Quite a romantic, your mother.

David: When she gets a couple of drinks in her—used to embarrass my father no end.

Manon: Must be nice, all the travelling she does.

David: Yeah. That generation lucked in. Property, investments, they have it all—

Manon: Mm, like Louis 16—*apres moi, le deluge*—no, I'm serious! Condos in the Bahamas, you name it, they've got it. They're not passing it on, they're using it up!

            Erin re-enters and watches them. They don't see her.

David: I know what you mean. Hey! What we need's some old style *ballad* justice, call it—redistribution?

Manon: Entrepreneurs with pistols: "stand and deliver!" So how's that going to work? If they've got it all, and we want it all too?

> *They are laughing, enjoying themselves. Erin comes and picks up her wine. She sits, sips. Silence.*

Erin: I like the wine, Dad. Dry but fruity. Just right on the palate.

David: Don't get used to it.

Erin: So, what are you talking about?

David: Oh, you know. The usual boring stuff. Work.

Erin: Nan looked weird, did you notice?

David: No.

Erin: Her face was all puffy. But the rest of her was—I don't know—small.

Manon: She's wonderful. Very feisty lady.

Erin: *(Beat.)* Thanks for correcting me, I feel much better about her now. I'm going to bed. Good night.

> *She takes her wine upstairs with her. Split scene, continuous action:*

David: She's been doing this lately, pushing the buttons.

Manon: How old is she?

David: Seventeen. Eighteen in a few months.

Erin: *(In her room.)* Celebrating my license? Sure, Dad.

Manon: Tough age.

> *Erin turns some music on in her room, begins to crank up the volume.*

David: She's great. Great. Hoping to head off to university—if she can settle on something. *(Irritated, calls:)* Erin! Keep it down, all right?

> *Erin, whose hand has remained poised on the volume, jerks it down to a bearable level.*

There's been the odd—hiccup. Along the way.

Erin: You should have *told* me…

David: You don't have kids, do you?

Manon: Nor a partner. Not even a pet. Too busy catching up.

David: Catching up?

Manon: Didn't know I used to be a high school teacher, did you?

David: What!

Manon: Oh, yes. Six years of it. Grades ten and eleven.

David: I can't see that, somehow.

Manon: Neither could I, in the end.

Erin: "The highwayman came riding…"

> *Erin lifts her glass in a toast.*

Manon: I don't know, I couldn't stand the apathy.

Erin: I wish. *(She drinks.)*

Manon: Most of them surrounded by riches and so damn— narrow… Is Erin—with you all the time?

David: Yeah, she's mine, she's here. My wife and I split about a year and a half ago—you didn't know?

Manon: No, I—

David: Steve never—?

Manon: Not a word. I didn't even know you had a daughter till today.

David: Really? Jesus.

          Erin has now picked up her phone and dialed a number.

Erin: *(Into phone.)* Hi, Mum? Yeah, I know it's late. Were you studying?

Manon: You and Steve known each other long?

David: Since university. He's a rocket, never married, no kids— he can just go straight for it.

Erin: *(Into phone.)* That sounds pretty boring.

Manon: Well, that's what I'm trying to do. Wish I'd started sooner.

David: You're good. You must have worked fast.

Erin: *(Into phone.)* Must be hard.

Manon: I've worked like a dog to get here.

David: My, uh—Susan's at law school. She suddenly—had to do it, too.

Erin: *(Into phone.)* Mum? There's a woman downstairs. With Dad. She works with them now. She's—

Manon: Did you mean what you said about the branch office? I mean, have you and Steve—ever considered a woman partner?

David: Well, we've never *talked* about it but—

Erin: *(Into phone.)* No, I just thought you'd want to know!

David: Once I move to Calgary, maybe that's what'll happen, Manon. Once you've been here a bit longer than six months?

Manon laughs and raises her glass.

Erin: *(Into phone.)* Never mind! I'm sorry I disturbed you. Good night!

> *Erin slams the phone down, goes to her computer to key in a search, as David's cellphone rings.*

David: *(Laughs.)* Like you said, it's a new world.

Erin: Man!

David: *(Into phone.)* Yeah? Sure. *(To Manon.)* It's Steve. Can you call Bob, in Calgary, their other line? Little crisis.

Erin: *(Looking into her screen.)* Highwaymen... "During times of upheaval..."

> *Manon digs her cellphone out of her purse and dials. The phone conversations can overlap:*

Manon: *(Into phone.)* Bob? What's up?

David: *(Into phone.)* She's on it, Steve.

Manon: *(Into phone.)* The due diligence review? I triple checked this morning.

David: *(Into phone.)* So it's costing—? That's too much, pal!

Manon: *(Into phone.)* On your e-mail. Sure they're panicked. Lawyers always are.

David: *(Into phone.)* Hey, what are you complaining about? You've got the glory work.

Manon: *(Into phone.)* —liabilities, no, no. Relax, Bob, it's clean. They can close the deal. No problem. Bye.

> *She hangs up. David gestures "just a second" at Manon.*

David: *(Into phone.)* Call me later tonight with that. Look, you can sleep in thirty years—quit griping.

> *David hangs up, and opens an appointment book to make some notes.*

Erin: *(Looking at her screen.)* "...and head for the road, to make their own way." Huh. Information highway, set *me* free!

Manon: *(Checking her watch.)* They're working late.

David: Don't make me feel guilty.

> *A glow begins to emanate from Erin's screen, and sound of approaching hoofbeats suddenly, under.*

Erin: *(Holding her head.)* Oh...wait... What's...?

> *The roar and flash of a musket blast fills the night sky. Erin recoils from her screen, and reaches out blindly. White light grows until, like a lightning bolt, and as if delivered by electrical charge—the man appears in the centre of the room. Erin comes to; they see each other. He draws a knife.*

Jemmy: Don't scream or I'll do ya.

> *Erin backs away, yells.*

Erin: Dad!

> *They listen, Jemmy with knife at the ready. No sound.*

Jemmy: I fancy 'e can't hear you.

> *Jemmy grabs Erin as she tries to bolt, and holds her against him, knife to her throat.*

Don't be afeared—I 'ave grievous need of quiet.

Erin: Please... Don't hurt me.

Jemmy: Promise you won't scream, then?

> *She nods. He lets her go. They stare at each other.*

David: *(Still writing.)* Sorry, Manon.

Manon: Not a problem.

Erin: You're not real. You're a dream. I can wake up any time.

Jemmy: Then I must behave, for I'd not wake to what I left for all the tea in China.

David: The environmental indemnities all checked out?

> *Jemmy picks up his hat, dusts it off on his leg, bows.*

Jemmy: Name's Jemmy.

Manon: There was just that last item.

Jemmy: James Ferguson, in the life. May I be seated? I find my legs rather—ah.

Erin: ...Shaking.

Jemmy: Indeed.

> *Pause. He sits, stunned.*

David: Make sure we're protecting this client.

Manon: We are.

Jemmy: Where am I?

Erin: ...Canada?

David: Great.

Jemmy: The colonies? Jesus, Mary and Joseph... Got any'fing to drink?

> *Erin gives him her wine and he downs it. Manon has come over to David as he finishes writing and his drink. He gestures at hers.*

David: Another? Want some ice?

Manon: Sure. Hey, we deserve a night off!

          They go off into the kitchen.

Jemmy: I was ridin' careful, knew somefin's up. Smelt it in the air,
          like, tinglin'—magic. Me darlin' mare, she's edgy too.
          Then—men and lanterns everywheres, I 'ears this shot
          an'—blazin', tearin' pain, like a lightning strike! She
          rears, I'm fallin'—I knows I've 'ad it, I knows they've got
          me—then I 'ears a voice! I 'ears "'ighway," I 'ears
          "free!"—an' I pray for it—pray for it 'ard, with all me
          guts— Then—blackness, rush o' noise, like bat's wings
          flappin', fallin' like a doxy's garters, like me ears is bein'
          torn off, then—Wham! I'm 'ere! Thought I'd snuffed it!

          Jemmy checks himself for bleeding musket holes.

          Must be one o' me nine lives! *(Grinning.)* Cor! New
          World, you say? Shoulda prayed more often!

          Jemmy struts and grins, pleased with himself.

Erin: Why were they shooting at you?

Jemmy: *(Conspiratorial.)* I rides like the devil, and I robs coaches,
          on the London-Dover road.

Erin: A—highwayman…!

Jemmy: Gentleman o' fortune, if you please. *(Bowing again.)*
          Capt'n Thunderball, at yer service.

          Erin laughs, delighted.

Erin: What happened to your eye?

Jemmy: An—accident. Tell ya the story some fine day.

Erin: How old are you? Forty?

Jemmy: I look so ancient?

Erin: Thirty-five? Thirty?

Jemmy: My life 'as been 'ard. But now—

Jemmy throws his frock coat off.

I'm free! Give us a kiss, then?

Jemmy takes Erin in his arms and kisses her, as Manon and David re-enter.

Manon: —No, I'm serious. You're lucky guys. This is a great set-up, David!

David: I've never felt my life was—lucky. I keep thinking I'm going to wake up one morning and it'll all be gone. Overnight. Some dumb mistake. Do you ever—?

Manon: *(Laughs.)* You should be on top of the world right now!

Erin, breathless, breaks away from Jemmy's kiss.

Jemmy: What's yer name?

Erin: …Erin.

David: Anyway. That's just me.

David and Manon settle again, with their drinks.

Jemmy: Where's your man, Erin?

Erin: You mean like, lover? I don't have one. Or want one.

Jemmy: You want *me* though, don't ya? 'Andsome devil like me?

Erin: *(Smiles.)* Well…

Jemmy: You saved me life, right enough! So give us another.

He kisses her again.

David: I was in another job too. Like you. With Shell Oil, in research.

Manon: Oh, yes?

David: Susan wanted security. I don't blame her, Erin needed it,
         but I was going nuts. Steve said, David, make a leap, take
         a chance! So I did. Susan was terrified. Getting Geoterme
         started was hell.

Jemmy: *(Lets Erin go, grinning.)* Like that, don't ya?

David: It's been pretty rough since we split. Erin blames her
         mother for the break-up, took it out on her by staying
         with me.

         Erin touches Jemmy's chest.

Erin: If you're just a dream, why are you so warm?

Jemmy: That's life. Feel it beatin'? Nuthin' like a little scrape wiv
         death to get the blood goin'!

David: Sorry, Manon, what am I boring you with all this for?

Manon: It's all right. I'm glad to know. I wondered.

         Erin reaches up to touch Jemmy's scar.

David: You know, Manon, Steve's a real— Sometimes he can be
         ruthless. He just wants to *win.* Whatever you do, don't
         tell him I said that.

Manon: *(Smiles.)* I won't.

David: Well, he's got family money, so he's safe.

         Jemmy pulls Erin close again.

Jemmy: You called me to ya, didn't you?

Manon: Is anybody? You know? That—"need-for-security"
         gene? It's not gender-based, David. I've never had it. I
         want to win too.

David: I know you do. It's very—attractive.

Manon: Think so?

Jemmy: (*Whispering into Erin's hair.*) You been waitin' fer me.

Erin: I think I have been.

David strokes Manon's cheek.

David: Manon, you're an amazing woman…

Erin sags against Jemmy, dizzy.

Erin: Everything's happening too fast, I'm— Ohh.

Jemmy: I'll be gentle as a lamb wiv ya first time, promise.

David: Beautiful…

David kisses Manon.

Erin: You're a dream, right? You came out of my head?

Jemmy: 'Deed I did. Straight out o' your 'ead—and into your life!

The highwayman music begins under, with a rhythm like repetitive hoofbeats. Jemmy picks Erin up and swings her up onto her bed.

You 'ave roads, you 'ave rich men—whatever the roads are, we'll ride 'em! Make our fortune!

Jemmy pulls his shirt off over his head.

Manon: I—I'm not too sure about the wisdom of this, Dave.

David: Neither am I…

Erin: (*Laughing.*)—Oh, my god, you're so—gorgeous!

Manon: But—

Jemmy: Seize the day, darlin'!

As Manon and David kiss again, Jemmy dives towards Erin and she shrieks and leaps off the bed, laughing. A

*bedroom lamp is knocked over and the light goes out.
Sound of crashing and loud, deep guttural yell as Erin
hits the floor, goes into seizure. David breaks away.*

David: Erin? That you?

Manon: What's—? David?

Another crash.

David: Oh, shit.

*David stumbles into Erin's room. Jemmy is in the
shadows. The others can't see him, but he is definitely
there.*

Sweetheart, sweetheart, s'ok, I'm here.

*David pulls a pillow off the bed and slips it under Erin's
head. Manon comes to the door, and watches, horrified
but fascinated. When the seizure ends, David rolls Erin
onto her side, strokes her hair. Manon stays in the
doorway.*

Shhhh. Shhhh. Poor baby, shhhh…

Manon: What's happening?

David: She's gonna be ok. It's ok. It's happened before—she has
epilepsy—maybe you could—

Manon: I'll just—shall I—?

Erin comes to and sees Manon. She hits out at her father.

Erin: Get her OUT of here! What's she doing here—Get her
AWAY from me!

Manon retreats, terrified. David cradles Erin's head.

David: Erin? Air? Shh…

Scene 3

> *Olivia alone in her house, same night, late. She is speaking the poem. David's cellphone is ringing and he enters to answer it.*

Olivia: "Over the cobbles he clattered and clashed in the dark inn-yard—"

David: *(Into phone.)* Yeah. *How* much?

Olivia: "And he tapped with his whip on the shutters, but all was locked and barred—"

David: *(Into phone.)* Steve, I'm stretched to the max now, you know that—*beyond.*

Olivia: "He whistled a tune to the window, and who should be waiting there—"

David: *(Into phone.)* We're *never* going to be in that league, no matter *what* we—

Olivia: "But the landlord's black-eyed daughter,
Bess, the landlord's daughter—
Plaiting a dark red love-knot into her long black hair..."

David: *(Into phone, looking very tired.)* Uhuh.

Olivia: I wanted *you*, Stan, not your money.

David: *(Into phone.)* Look. It's a huge whack of cash. I can't promise—

Olivia: Not the house. Not the trips we saved for, that I take, alone.

David: *(Into phone.)* I'll try! I don't know how, but I'll try!

Olivia: I wanted *you.*

> *As David hangs up, Olivia takes a couple of pills, washing them down with distaste.*

Scene 4

> *Living room, as Erin enters from her bedroom, the next morning. David looks as if he hasn't slept.*

David: Ok, you're seeing her at eleven, and the CAT scan's at three. Oh. I asked about your job?—don't hate me, sweetie. It's the noise and frenetic pace I'm thinking of. And those hot grills… She thinks you should stop for a bit.

Erin: Did you tell her I got my license?

David: Well, there's that. I'm sorry, but—until they know what's going on—she said you shouldn't be driving either.

Erin: I knew it.

David: Just for a while.

Erin: That's a lie! I have to be two years seizure-free! And I need that job. I need my own money! Otherwise, you have to know what it's for all the time and I—

David: Ok, Erin, ok, we'll figure something out… For now, she wants to up the dosage of Dilantin. Do a few more tests. All right?

> *Pause. Erin is looking at the floor. She is furious.*

Erin: That stuff makes me sick, Dad.

David: You can't start fighting this—come on, now.

Erin: It makes my gums bleed. I feel like I'm behind glass, nothing's real. *(Beat.)* I stopped taking them. Last month.

David: You *what?*

Erin: I'm not going to live my whole life—

David: You have to. You *have* to, Erin, don't you understand?
          After all this time? *(Beat.)* Tell her. I can't believe you've
          done this.

Erin: I hate this! It's like I'm in prison, inside my own head! I'll
          never be able to do *any*thing my whole life.

David: You know it's connected with stress and fatigue—

Erin: You're controlling me!

David: I'm not!

Erin: At least without pills I *feel* things. I cry and laugh and—

David: —and have seizures, yeah, and over-react—

Erin: *(Explosive.)* You don't understand *any*thing! *(Pause.)*
          Have you been seeing that woman and didn't tell me?

David: No, I—we've become friends, I told you that.

Erin: Why did you let her watch me?

David: She didn't—

Erin: She was right there, gawking at me! In my own room!

David: Look, Erin—

Erin: —I called Mum. I told her she was here.

David: Why'd you do that?

Erin: Because!

          David tries to hold her but she flinches away.

          So are we going, or what? I don't want you to wait. Just—
          come back when they're finished. You'll be here, right?
          Working, with her?

          He nods.

          It's like an enemy, you know. My worst enemy.

Scene 5

> *At Olivia's house in the country, later that day. Olivia is bringing in tea and cookies.*

Olivia: —it's wonderful you're here. Did you see the front garden on your way in?

David: Bit jungly.

Olivia: I like it, keeps the weeds down. Or at least you don't notice them as much.

David: Mum. Erin's had a seizure.

Olivia: What? Oh, no…

David: She's at the hospital. Tests. I don't know what's going on.

Olivia: Oh, I'm *so* sorry. I'm worried about her, David. She's too serious for her age.

David: Yeah, well. We just have to get through it.

> *She has offered him a cookie. He examines it.*

…How long have you had these?

Olivia: I don't know! Are you complaining about my food now? Honestly, you've become so fussy!

David: They're beyond stale, Mum. They're—indescribable.

Olivia: Give me that.

> *She moves the plate to the other side of the room.*

There. Happy?

> *She returns to sit with him again.*

You're turning into such an old woman—you know, you really should leave that to me. *(Beat.)* Why didn't you tell me over the phone?

David: I wanted to see you! Is that so odd?

Olivia: Honestly? Yes. But I try not to mind; I know you're busy.
            The forties are hell. Your father was a bear in a hornet's
            nest every day for ten years. I just hope I'm still around
            when you return to the human race.

David: They tell you, be an entrepreneur—so I'm running as fast
            as I can. Put away for retirement's the new one—but I've
            started too late. What's the use?

Olivia: I've been trying to tell you...

David: I know, but there's no cash, Mum. Everything's tied up
            in—

Olivia: You think *we* didn't feel this way? You're in the what-do-
            they-call-it?—boomer bulge. You'll be fine. It's Erin you
            should be worried about. I don't know what's going to
            happen to her lot.

David: Mum, I *am*. I'm worried about everything.

Olivia: This is what you *wanted*. That's what you kept telling me.

David: I don't know if I can keep it up.

Olivia: You'll never get anywhere if you don't stick with
            something.

David: You don't get it! People are changing all the time. We put
            on new suits, new smiles, every day, running scared—
            we're just plain running. All the fucking time.

Olivia: Don't be like that.

David: Sorry.

            There is silence. Olivia sips her tea. David fidgets, then:

David: Look, Mum... I'm in a bit of a jam. Steve's in Calgary, as
            you know, and uh—getting this new office outfitted is,
            well—I was wondering—

Olivia: I knew it. It's money. That's why you're here.

David: I was just thinking—a loan. For a short period. We're going to make a killing out there. It's just a short-term cash problem I'm juggling. And I thought—maybe an advance on—god, I hate saying this—on my…inheritance? I mean—

Olivia: How do you know I've left you anything?

            David is stunned. Olivia gets to her feet.

            I don't know what comes over me sometimes. We've never done this, as a family, we've never talked about anything other than the weather and gardens and vacations—but I'm afraid I'll run out of time if I don't speak now—

David: Mum, what are you talking about?

Olivia: *(With rising intensity.)* If I become unable to cope, do something. Don't let them take me away.

David: What do you mean, do something? What could I do?

Olivia: I will not end my life catatonic in some institution, with young well-meaning Christians yammering at me and holding my hand. With none of my things around me and plastic pants to hold my urine and you and Erin visiting me on Sundays, when you can tear yourselves away.

David: Don't. This is terrible.

Olivia: Yes, it is. I'd rather be dead. Are you listening to me? I'd rather be dead than like that.

David: God, Mum.

Olivia: I'm staying here, in this old house, with my jungly garden, and I'm not going to budge. Period!

David: …Ok.

Olivia: Promise me.

David: Ok. I promise. I do!

Olivia: (Beat.) What would your father have thought of that?

David: He'd have left the room five minutes ago.

Olivia: He would have. Oh, we should be thinking about Erin, not ourselves.

David: It's her own doing, Mum. She stopped taking her medication.

Olivia: Why?

David: I don't know. Why do we do anything? I don't know.

Olivia: I remember her as such a sunny little girl.

David: *You* trying to make me feel guilty too?

Olivia: Of course not!

Pause. Olivia picks up her tea.

David: I hate to go back to it, Mum, but—

Olivia: What?

David: Well, what if you suddenly—*can't* cope? I don't like to be blunt, but—it can happen quickly. If you won't sell the house, and if I haven't been able to keep the business going—do you see? I won't be *able* to do anything.

Olivia: I have investments. Some. The government took a huge amount after Stan…died, but.

David: Dad left you in pretty good shape, didn't he?

Olivia: Well, that's what worrying me. I don't really *know*. Oh, it's ridiculous, but I've never had to think about all this before…

David: It's terrible, I know.

Olivia: Try to see it from my point of view. If I give you money, what happens if you lose it? Not on purpose—but in a volatile market, or whatever it is. I'd have nothing to live on.

David: I'm not asking for a lot.

Olivia: Yes, dear, you are. I've got to take care of myself. No, I have to. It's safer.

David looks away. He is finding this very hurtful.

Your father and I bailed you out not once, but twice, I hope you remember? We paid off your loans, then helped you set Geoterme up—well, didn't we?

David: Yeah.

Olivia: Then you should know. Before he died. He said that was the last time, that you'd have to swim on your own from now on. Well, I jolly well wish you'd learn to.

David is ashamed and, underneath that, very angry.

You must think I'm a terrible old skinflint. Oh, this is dreadful. I so wish you hadn't asked me.

David: So do I. Believe me.

Olivia, now full of remorse, returns to sit with him.

Olivia: You need a woman in your life. It can't be easy, coping alone. And now this.

David: Erin's a good kid. A *great* kid.

Olivia: You're still helping Susan, I'll bet.

He nods.

Oh, David, why!

David: She's at law school, Mum. She's got no income yet—

Olivia: And then you complain—! How you managed to spend
            so much money when you were together and *still*
            consider yourself a young radical, I don't know.

David: It's complicated. I don't want to get into it.

Olivia: *(Gently.)* She's not coming back, David.

David: Can we get off this subject, please?

Olivia: I think we'd better.

David: *(Beat.)* I'd better get going.

Olivia: Wait. Oh, dear. I don't mean to stick my nose in your
            business. I'm just concerned. You seem so—unhappy.

David: Yeah, well, me and thousands of others.

Olivia: Your father used to say that. He'd mutter "men live lives
            of quiet desperation," and I'd want to say to him, "and
            why do women stand for it?"

David: *(Quietly.)* Why didn't you?

Olivia: I don't know. Oh, David. If I can't trust you, I can't trust
            anyone. I've been feeling uneasy about Henry, you
            know, our investment counsellor? His eyes have gone
            all—shifty—when he looks at me.

David: I don't know anything about your investments.

Olivia: I know, but—well, I'm just wondering now if you could
            take a look. Maybe I'll find that I have more than I know.
            And that I'll be *able* to help you.

David: You'd have to call your bank.

Olivia: I will. I can do all that. Get them to give you full access,
            whatever you need.

David: Then—yeah, of course, if it'll help.

Olivia: I've been neglectful of your father's stocks, in particular;
            the cancer's been a distraction, to say the least. But
            David—you will be careful, won't you?

David: Of *course* I will. Of *course*.

Olivia: Fine.

            He kisses her, turns to go.

            David?

            He turns back.

            No, nothing. Go on, dear.

            He goes.

Olivia: *(To herself.)* Am I worth more to you dead than alive…?

Scene 6

            That afternoon. Manon is working on a file.

Manon: *(On phone.)* Let me run it past Mr. Dafoe, and I'll get back
            to you. Great, Mr. Seymour. Goodbye.

            David enters with Erin, who is in a foul mood.

Erin: —I've got to take a shower. My hair's disgusting from the
            goo.

David: Maybe you should lie down for a bit, eh?

Erin: I'll do what I want!

            She slams into her room and flings herself on her bed.

Manon: I—just got off the phone with Seymour, the airport
            cleanup? They've had a lower bid. Do you want me
            to—?

David: Aaach! The subcontractors are killing us!

Manon: I'm going to head out there, then, check it out.

David: Go lower if you have to. Damn! We need that job.

Manon: Is Erin—ok?

David: She will be.

Manon: Are you?

David: Ditto. Tough day, poor kid. They bring on a seizure so they can watch, figure out what's happening.

Manon: I went home last night feeling so terrible. Like I'd invaded—

David: No, no. Not your fault.

Manon: It's very scary.

David: It was under control but... Teenagers. Have to assert their independence, you know? She's had episodes of acting out—cutting herself.

Manon: Cutting?

David: That's over, but. Shit.

Manon: *(Beat.)* Is this going to work? I mean, my being here?

David: Of course.

Manon: It's just—

David: She's coming up to exams, final year—it's nerves. She understands about the business—she knows how important the next few months are. It's fine.

Manon: I hope so. I mean—

David: The biggest problem's the changeover, keeping the cash flowing. I shouldn't be telling you that, but. Handle Seymour carefully, ok?

She nods and turns to go, then back.

Manon: I—need to get it out in the open, Dave. I've been thinking about it all night.

David: …Me too.

Manon: Not at the office, I don't think, do you?

David: Well. This isn't really the office, it's still my home. But, fine. I'd never—

Manon: I know you wouldn't.

David: What happened has nothing to do with us, how I feel about you—

Manon: I know, but… It's—overwhelming, all mixed up like this with Erin.

David: I guess.

Manon: Can we—let it happen, or not? Can we—wait and see? I mean—

David: 'Course we can. Of course. No worries.

Manon: Thanks.

                 As she's almost out the door:

David: Manon. Don't lose them.

Scene 7

                 That night. David making a call on his cellphone, in the "office."

David: (*Into phone.*) Susan. I know Erin called you last night. Pretty late, we'd been celebrating. Her license, didn't she tell you? Yeah, it's wonderful but—shortlived, I'm afraid: she had a seizure. No, her medication. She'd been experimenting, not taking it. I know. Listen, I wanted to explain about... I know, no ties, but... Suze. You know I still wish... Well, sorry, but I do. The company's doing great— No, I'm happy to help. Don't feel guilty, I wish you wouldn't... So you're doing well? Enjoying it? You're going to be a fine lawyer... Suze, Erin— exaggerates, you know that. *(Into empty phone line.)* — Susan?

> *Erin lying on her bed. Jemmy is in Erin's room, sitting at the computer, face close to the screen, engrossed. He has her Walkman on.*

Jemmy: *(Knocking on computer screen.)* Hey! When's this fing goin' to do somefin' else?

> *David sighs, hangs up, and exits.*

Erin: When are you going back?

Jemmy: You know what they'd do to me if I went back. *(He draws a finger across his throat.)* Kkkkrit! Don't want thet, do ya?

Erin: I don't know what I want. *(Beat.)* Why are you called Captain Thunderball?

Jemmy: Speed I ride. I prefers the ambush—drop on 'em like a clap of thunder from the sky, down from a hilltop— wham!

Erin: Why do you steal?

Jemmy: Adventure. Danger. I loves the chase. An' the money, o' course. I'm the best on the road.

Erin: How many of you are there?

Jemmy: Cor, it's a epidemic. Youngest sons o' merchants, most o' us—oldest son inherits. Bugger thet. Grow up thinkin' about money, never able to expect any as your right? So you decide to *take*. What do they expect? 'Course, bein' famous ain't no 'ardship. Bein' robbed by Captain Thunderball's the thrill of a lifetime!

He pinches her.

Erin: Ow! You know, you're not at all what Nan imagines.

Jemmy: Oo's thet?

Erin: My grandmother. She thinks highwaymen are gentle-men, fallen on hard times, that you're wild but kind. She gets tears in her eyes when she thinks of your life.

Jemmy: Ha! She wants me in 'er bed!

Erin: Don't be gross.

Jemmy: Ah, she does. You don't know nuffin' yet. There's women fallin' at our feet left an' right. 'Undreds o' songs written 'bout us. An' why do you fink thet is?

Erin: I don't know. People want to think there's someone who doesn't have to follow rules?

Jemmy: Yeah! An' you don't 'ave to neither.

Erin: Wanna make a bet?

Jemmy: I've been finkin'. I'm finkin' you and me'll get ready for a journey. Little cash, little robbery, tide us over. Stand and deliver!

         He pulls a coin out from behind her ear. She laughs.

         What's this, then? Sleight o 'and, 'and in pocket, bob's yer uncle, ha! Got to be quick in this trade. Come on, can't 'ave you lyin' about, doin' nothin' but lustin' after me.

         He yanks her to her feet, slaps her bum.

         Get on me back. We'll go fer a ride. See if we can find somefin' interestin'.

Erin: Jemmy…

         He gallops them out to the "office."

Jemmy: Whoo hooo!

Erin: (*Laughing.*) Be quiet.

Jemmy: What's all this, then? Fancy.

Erin: It's rented. I hate it.

Jemmy: "Rented?"

Erin: Most of it Dad doesn't own, just has it for show.

> *Jemmy sets her down.*

Jemmy: I tried to catch meself a wife thet way once. Hired a fine
         carriage, took 'er out in it, we jaunted off to one pub arter
         another and finally a swanky coachin'-inn. I got 'er into
         bed—and found out she'd told me she was well-to-do in
         order to catch 'ersel' an 'usband, and she'd 'eard *I* was
         rich! So we flummoxed each *other!* Ha ha!

Erin: (*Amazed.*) Really?

Jemmy: Yeah, really! See, I recken I knows yer problem. Like a
         mouse in the 'ouse, you are. Got to be like Mary Frith, she
         works the roads, an' she's demned good at it—call ya the
         Roarin' Girl, shall I? Like the sound o' thet?

> *He roars, beats his chest.*

         Rooooaar-in'!

Erin: (*Laughs.*) You're crazy. What are we doing?

Jemmy: (*Leaping to the top of David's desk.*) Agh, where's me darlin'
         mare? I'm stagnatin' 'ere!

Erin: Shh! Dad's gone to bed—he'll hear us.

Jemmy: 'E can't 'ear a fing.

> *Jemmy scratches his head energetically.*

Aaaarrrhhh! Little buggers, they're killin' me. Wot you lookin' at me so queer for?

Erin: Nothing about you is what I thought. You're so real, but—how could I have made you up?

Jemmy: We're two sides o' one coin. I'm all yours, Erin. I *am* you, ha!

He sees Manon's computer and sits down at it.

These fings're a spree. I can't get enough of 'em! Show me again wot the next bit is?

Erin: Click on that.

Jemmy: Oh, yeah, 'at's it.

Erin: We shouldn't do this. She's probably got a secret password.

Jemmy: I'm an expert cracksman. Watch.

He cracks his knuckles, puts his ear up against the computer screen, listening, then hits a few keys.

Ha ha! We're in.

Erin: Oh, this is spooky…

Jemmy: (*Looking at screen.*) 'Ere comes somefin'. Wot now?

Erin: There's new messages. Click on ok.

Jemmy: Wot's that say, then?

Erin: (*Reading.*) It's from Steve. Dad's partner. "Trust me. You won't regret it." I don't want to look at this.

Jemmy: Wot's that bit?

Erin: Let's see? …What she wrote to him, earlier.

She wants to disconnect but it catches her eye.

Erin: (*Reading.*) "David's on top of everything, don't worry…
          There *is* a lot to—juggle, it's not the easiest atmosphere…
          His daughter…seizure"—Shit! "If there's something
          going on between you and David, don't put me in the
          middle, Steve, because that's not fair."

          She disconnects them.

Jemmy: Oy!

Erin: I don't want to know this.

          Jemmy pinches her hard.

          Ow! That hurts!

Jemmy: If you can't be bothered to watch yer tail, then y'er gonna
          get it chewed off, an' you deserve it. I recken she's findin'
          out which side 'er bread is buttered.

Erin: Steve's his partner!

Jemmy: Exactly. I 'ad a partner once, meself. Caught 'im stealin'
          my share one night when 'e thought I was sleepin'.

Erin: What happened to him?

Jemmy: (*Beat.*) We ain't partners no more.

          Jemmy grins.

Erin: You don't steal from the rich to give to the poor, either,
          do you?

Jemmy: Pff! Wot's the point o' thet?

Erin: You didn't kill him, did you? Your partner?

Jemmy: What if I did? I'm not the patient type, 'case you 'adn't
          noticed. If I wants somefin', I goes for it, yeah? Blaze o'
          lightnin' forkin' through the sky—ziiiit! Hit the ground!
          Flames!

Erin: …That's what it was.

Jemmy: Wot?

Erin: Today. At the hospital. That's what I saw. Blazing light…

Jemmy: In yer fit?

Erin: Everything was—purple. Dark. You were there. We were together, riding down a road.

Jemmy: 'At's it, we was.

Erin: There were tears in my eyes, we were galloping so fast, and it was cold… I had to get back somewhere before something terrible happened. There was this huge face in the sky… Then, lightning—and fire, running through me.

Jemmy: 'At's awful poetic, Erin. Luvly.

Erin: I thought I was dying.

Jemmy: Did ya, now? An' you never believed it'd 'appen to you, did ya?

Erin: No… It was…freezing cold. Like a huge—empty space, and this weight, on my chest… It felt easier…to let go…

          She is crying now, frightened.

          It's never been like that before… I'm so scared. What's happening, Jemmy?

Jemmy: Don't go all soft on me, eh? I needs a partner, strong and free. A Roarin' Girl. You called me to ya. You better be up to it. Gimme yer 'and now. Gimme it!

          He takes Erin's hand, roughly.

          'At's it. We'll let you get yer ridin' legs, bring you back, safe and sound, for a little while. Just a little canter. The road? Yer freedom? Can't ya feel it comin'? No one ever said it was goin' to be easy.

Erin: Jemmy...

            Flashes of yellow light through red, like lights flashing
            on closed eyelids, as room darkens. Erin yells as the
            seizure begins, sounds of thrashing.

Scene 8

            The next afternoon, in the "office." Manon is at her
            computer, checking her e-mail. She frowns.

Manon: *(To herself.)* What's going on—? *(Keying in.)* I never got
            this... Who...?

            Erin enters. Manon stops, they look at each other.

Erin: Where's Dad?

Manon: Um—

Erin: I guess he's not here.

Manon: No. He asked me to stay till you got home. He was
            worried—

Erin: He knew where I was. I was at school. I was studying.

Manon: Erin? I hope—this isn't going to be too distracting for
            you. Me being here. I know it's—

Erin: It's what Dad wants.

Manon: I'm—very sorry, about the other night.

Erin: Doesn't matter.

Manon: It does, to me.

Erin: *(Suddenly fierce.)* I really don't like talking about it, okay?

Manon: Well. Right. *(Gathering together her things.)* I have to meet
            him. He's finishing up a presentation at the airport. He—

asked me to tell you to go ahead with dinner. There's a casserole in the fridge you can just heat up. And the salad from last night.

Erin: He told you to tell me that? I can't believe this!

She picks up David's phone and dials.

(Into phone.) Nan? Hi, it's Erin. Remember you said you'd like me to visit? Well I'd like to—as soon as possible. *(Looking at Manon.)* Yeah, Dad thinks it's a good idea. I can study. What time tomorrow? Great. See you then. *(Hangs up. To Manon:)* Would you please make sure my father gets that message?

Manon: Erin.

Erin: What?

Manon: I'm not a servant, all right? Let's get that straight.

Erin: Never thought you were.

Manon looks away first. Erin feels Jemmy's presence. It makes her feel stronger.

You don't like me, do you? You think I'm a freak. When you look at me, you look scared.

Manon: Don't be ridiculous. Why would I be scared of you?

Erin: I don't know. That's what I keep wondering.

Manon: Look, I just want to be able to do my job without—

Erin: You just want to go to bed with my father.

Manon: How dare you!

Erin, feeling Jemmy, smiles to herself. Jemmy grins.

When did you go into my computer and read my messages?

Erin: I don't know what you're talking about.

Manon: Oh, yes, you do. That's—stealing. It's private.

Erin: Like my room is private? In my house? Private like that?

Manon: I've already said I'm sorry. It's not me that's brought this situation about. There's nothing further I can do, is there? Short of—

Jemmy: Slashin' yer wrists?

Manon silences herself. She is shaking.

Manon: I hope you find some good studying time.

Erin: I will.

Manon picks up her briefcase and exits.

Jemmy: Ha ha…

Erin: …Bye bye.

Crossfade to Olivia's, as verse is heard. She is entering, with her purse. She takes an envelope of money from the purse and files it on her desk. She exits, moving slowly, in pain.

Voice: (*Sings.*) "Yet if they press me sharply,
                 and harry me through the day…
             Look for me by moonlight,
             Watch for me by the moonlight,
             I'll come to thee by the moonlight—
             Though hell should bar the way."

Scene 9

That night, late. The office. Erin is lying on Manon's desk, with Jemmy, who is swigging from a bottle of whisky. He begins to sing to a raucous tune, jarring against the ballad verse, and lights up during it.

Jemmy: (*Sings.*) "Nor beg nor cheat will I—I scorn the same,
         But while I live, maintain a soldier's name.
         I'll purse it, I—the Highway is my Hope!
         His heart's not great that fears a little rope."

> *He makes a face and gesture, as of being violently hung.*

Gaaa!

> *He laughs uproariously. He has his hand inside her shirt; she is very turned on.*

Like thet, don't ya?

Erin: Yeah… He shouldn't be this late. He must be with her, in the car. They must have stopped. They must be—

Jemmy: Don't be jealous o' yer old man. Thet's sick.

> *She pushes his hand away.*

Erin: I just care about him, I just worry what he's doing. I bet she didn't even tell him I'm going to Nan's.

Jemmy: Ha! 'Ere's wot I 'fink. 'E doesn't notice ya no more. 'E's pushin' you outta yer own 'ome—an' you should make 'im regret it!

> *He walks away from the desk. His knife is lying beside Erin. She looks at it.*

Did I drop thet? No, no, 'at's a nice piece o' work thet is. You 'ave a look, if you like. You know, most o' the time 'e 'as you 'oled up in yer room like a criminal. Shame. Leaves you on yer own—

> *She picks up the knife, studies it.*

Erin: I wanted him to.

Jemmy: No, you didn't, not really. Why don't 'e know thet? Eh? 'E's not really listenin', is 'e?

Erin: He's got a lot on his mind.

Jemmy: Oh, an' you don't?

Erin: Don't make fun of me.

Jemmy: I'm takin' you ever so serious, Erin. What's 'e want? Money? Don't fink so—'e keeps puttin' it elsewhere soon as 'e gets it.

Erin: I don't know.

Jemmy: Not you, thet's obvious. You said y'er afraid, 'fraid o' pain? 'Fraid o' dyin'? Let's cogitate on that. Why should death bother ya? It's a kind o' ecstasy. If you go right. Easy as gallopin' down a road; you reach the end, road stops, ya falls over the edge, an' then—ziiit—out! *(Takes his knife from her.)* Eh? It's resistance thet's exhaustin'. Why do you do thet, Erin?

Erin: I don't know what you're talking about. I—

         He stabs his knife violently into the desk. She leaps to her feet, scared.

Jemmy: Don't make me 'ang around, gettin' bored! You gonna be a Mary Frith—a Roarin' Girl—or ya gonna be dragged along fer the ride like a sack o' mouldy taters? *(Looks at her.)* Ha! Look at yer white face! Wot'd you 'fink I was goin' to do?

Erin: I'm not afraid of you.

Jemmy: Oh. You are. *(Beat.)* You don't 'ave a clue, do ya? You 'ave no idea 'oo I am.

         He puts his knife down again, gestures to it.

         Release the pressure, Erin. I dare ya.

         She goes to pick up the knife, then stops.

         Why'd you stop?

Erin: Because.

Jemmy: It's been a long time, eh? Thet little bliss. Just a little cut. That breath before the blood comes, before the pain comes. It's an ecstasy, ain't it? Just a little wound, a little mouth openin', little red lips whisperin' "set me free…"

Erin: Will it make you leave me alone?

Jemmy: That's what you want?

> *Erin pulls up her sleeve and holds the knife against her upper arm. As she begins to cut herself, the lights go to black.*

Voice: (*Sings.*) "He loosened her hair i' the casement.
            His face burnt like a brand
         As the black cascade of perfume
            came tumbling over his breast;
         And he kissed its waves in the moonlight,
         Oh, sweet black waves in the moonlight
         Then he tugged at his reins in the moonlight,
            and galloped away to the West.

         END OF ACT I

Act Two

Lights up at Olivia's. Two days later. Olivia and Erin are repotting houseplants.

Olivia: You came so laden with computers and Walkmans—when I was a young girl, travelling, I had a cardboard suitcase and a hat. *(Stops, looks at her.)* You like it out here, don't you? You don't miss your friends?

Erin: I wanted to get away from a bunch of things. I'm kind of a loner, Nan.

Olivia: I know. I'm not sure I shouldn't be worried about that, too.

Erin: Don't bother.

Olivia: I think you don't get outside enough. You're very pale.

Erin: I have to study, 'cause I have to do well, and I can't study at home—feels like the walls are getting smaller.

Pause. Olivia looks at her with worry, then back to what she's doing.

Olivia: You're going to have to tell me if you're not feeling well, you know.

Erin: I will.

Olivia: I'm a bit nervous about it, I have to admit.

Erin: Dad didn't want me to come here right now.

Olivia:　I thought you said—

Erin:　Sorry. We're sort of fighting.

Olivia:　Oh, Erin. I don't like to feel you've put me between you…

Erin:　He's ok about it now. He's in the middle of some big proposal, anyway. It makes him crazy.

Olivia:　*(Handing a plant to Erin.)* Here, this fellow needs a new home. Been in the same place too long. Use lots of this good soil.

Erin:　Ok.

　　　　She winces as she lifts the pot. Olivia sees this and frowns.

Olivia:　Anything wrong?

Erin:　Nothing.

Olivia:　Have you hurt yourself?

Erin:　No. Why don't you sing anymore, Nan?

Olivia:　Oh, good heavens. My voice has gotten far too quavery to be unleashed in public. *You're* the one that should be singing. You've a lovely voice.

Erin:　I suck. No, seriously.

Olivia:　You're just shy. You'll come into your own… Have you ever wanted to live in the country?

Erin:　I've never thought about it. *(Beat.)* Nan? Are you rich?

Olivia:　I most certainly am not! Whatever gave you that idea?

Erin:　Well, this house. And—

Olivia:　Your grandfather and I worked hard for what we have.

Erin: But—you never worked, did you?

Olivia: I did! I raised your father, kept a home and a marriage. I know those things are out of fashion now. A woman's supposed to do them in her sleep while she's thinking about navigational equipment or whatever it is her life is supposed to be really about.

Erin: It's not enough, though.

Olivia: Oh, I know, dear. It's survival of the fittest for all of you. I don't know where we went wrong.

Erin: No, I mean, those aren't choices, any of them. Be a workaholic, or be a mother—or be both and go nuts.

Olivia: I don't think I thought about things like this at your age.

Erin: Why not?

Olivia: I don't know why not. Life's very—complicated now. Seems all about acquiring, and that makes people heartless, and it fills me with dread. It's what life was like in the war. Demonize the different, ignore the elderly—

Erin: You weren't in the war.

Olivia: Oh, yes, I was. I was a young girl, younger than you are, but boys went away and didn't come back. My cousin. Two uncles. I saw what it did to my parents. You don't have to *live* something to *feel* it, in your soul—people don't seem to know that anymore. And that's frightening, too.

Erin: ...Are you scared, Nan? Of death? Maybe you don't want to talk about it...

Olivia: Of course I don't. Who does? Are you asking because—

Erin: I don't know why. You don't have to. Never mind.

    Pause.

Olivia: Yes, I'm scared. Like a chill wind down my spine
           whenever I think of it, because it's coming, and it's—
           unknowable. We have no idea what to expect, none at all,
           no matter what the churches say. When you're young,
           even if you're not—completely well, you think—that
           death can't happen to you. It's why young people are
           more foolhardy, perhaps. They're not yet fully
           connected, to everything that's here, everything they
           have. It doesn't yet mean very much. Maybe that's rather
           fanciful—

Erin: No, it's not. Go on.

Olivia: Then at my age...? Especially if there's pain, it can
           seem—seductive. A friend. And I'm realizing you'd
           better learn to embrace it, because you can't sidestep
           death, it's not going away, and if you can't get a sort of a
           grip on this unknowable thing, then you're going to be in
           a terrible state—Stan was in such a terrible state... (*Looks
           at Erin, worried.*) That's probably more than you wanted
           to know, isn't it? ...Erin? There are so many ways you
           can do what you want with your life. Don't let this small
           setback stop you.

Erin: It's not small. I don't want to spend my life watching
           everyone else have a good time, being afraid to do
           anything. Like, in that ballad—why does she have to die
           in her bedroom, for the highwayman?

Olivia: Well, because she loves him. She wants him to be free.

Erin: She should be riding, getting away—!

Olivia: They've tied her up. She can't get free. But she thinks, at
           least I can help *him.*

Erin: No, I think he wants her dead—it makes him excited, her
           finger on the trigger, turned against herself.

Olivia: What do you mean, dear?

Erin: He wants to see how far he can make her go. He's a thief
           and a murderer! Why don't songs tell the truth!

Olivia: Erin?

> *Erin feels Jemmy's presence suddenly in Olivia's house.*
> *Olivia does not see him.*

Erin: …Sorry. I'm sorry, Nan.

Olivia: Something's troubling you, I can feel it. What *is* it, dear?

Erin: Nothing.

> *Olivia regards Erin with consternation.*

Olivia: I think of that ballad as rather like myth. It satisfies some need, it has a deeper meaning. I know your father laughs at me *and* my imagination, but when I want to understand something, I do go back to literature. Writers are the only visionaries I trust, I'm afraid. Oh.

> *Olivia suddenly winces, in intense pain.*

Erin: You ok?

Olivia: Oh. No. Could you—my pills? They're right there, oh.

> *Erin gets Olivia her the pills, and helps her take them.*
> *As Olivia speaks, Erins looks straight at Jemmy.*

Oh, Erin… Just give me a second. There's great forces that pass through us, and we need to be…big enough for them… Almost over. Ride it out.

Scene 11

> *Evening, David and Manon in the "office."*

David: Steve should be in Yellowknife by now. Lucky dog. I'd rather be travelling than this—waiting! Why doesn't he phone?

Manon: Call him.

> *David does, on his cellphone.*

Oh, my feet hurt. Do you mind if I—?

David: Go ahead.

She takes her shoes off.

He's not answering. Must have turned it off. Damn!

Manon: He may be trying to catch some sleep… Dave? What's wrong?

David: Maybe this sounds nuts, but—can I run something past you?

Manon: Sure.

David: Well. Something's going on with Steve. You noticed anything?

Manon: Like what?

David: The past couple of months, he'd send you out on site, not even asking me if—

Manon: You guys need elbow room to work on new contracts. That's what he said.

David: And now that he's in Calgary, he's calling you instead of me—I mean, it's my company too!

Manon: Come on, that's a bit—paranoid, isn't it? I set up that particular contract for him. I'm the easiest person to ask.

David: Yeah. You're right. You're right. Sorry to do that to you.

Manon: It's ok.

David: …I've been hanging on, you know, waiting? I'm forty-five years old, I don't have forever—I can't go at this half-assed. I've got to be there, every minute! I thought Erin understood, but she's playing these power games and— Ah, she's still a kid. I'm being a jerk. But I can't afford for her to be sick any more! Does that sound as terrible as it feels?

Manon: Not to me.

David: I've never said that to anyone. I feel like a traitor.

Manon: Dave, you're a great dad. I saw a lot of parents in action, when I was teaching? You guys really have something. Actually? I think she's very protective of you.

David: Think so? *(Beat.)* I heard a… The other day, on the radio? This guy, some yuppie with a BMW, you know, wife with a high-powered job, two kids under three. He was dropping the kids off that morning at daycare, whatever, and there was this deadline he was thinking about, you know, obsessing over. He got to work and it was go go go all day, all went well, he went out for a beer with the guys at 5:00 to celebrate, cool off—it was sweltering hot—and he remembered it was his turn to pick the kids up too 'cause his wife had flown out earlier to—

Manon: Dave?

David: I'm almost finished. So he went to his car, probably whistling, half-cut maybe, keys in hand. When he opened his door, he saw the kids, the little babies—they were still strapped in to their car seats. The windows were closed tight. He'd— He'd forgotten… They'd been there all… Jesus.

Manon: Hey.

        He turns away, overcome.

        You going to be ok?

David: I don't think so, no. I don't think I am.

        In her house, Olivia enters in her nightgown, and looks out at the night. Manon goes to David.

Manon: David… Erin's safe. She's all right.

David: My chest hurts, it's so tight.

Manon: You've got to ride it easier, David. Trust the fates.

David: I can't. The business—

Manon: What's the worst that can happen? The bottom could
drop out. Signs seem to say that it won't. Steve's more
aggressive, he likes the chase, so that's a given. He can
go after them, but it needs you to land them. That's
what makes you guys a great team. The one thing I
never want to happen?—is to have to take sides,
between you.

David: Has Steve—?

Manon: No. But—I don't know. I just don't want us to get too big
too fast. I can't believe I said that.

David: ...I was at the bank the other day, for my mother? She's
got stocks and bonds. IBM, Xerox. I mean, those were
the days to get in on the ground floor. My dad was
pretty shrewd. He slaved his guts out. Nine months
retired, then wham. He's dead. Sometimes I get so
angry at her, never worked a day in her life, how could
she tell me that she's leaving me—nothing... When
she...has so much...

  Pause.

I don't know why I told you all that.

Manon: It's ok. It's ok.

David: ...Remember that ballad she was going on about? About
the highwayman?

Manon: Yes?

David: There's this one line I always—it scared me when I was a
kid—now the stupid thing's come back to me, and I
can't—shake it.

Manon: What is it?

David: Something about shooting him, "Down like a dog on the highway. And he...lay in his blood on the highway, with a bunch of lace at his throat."

Manon: That's how he dies?

David: He mistimes everything. Goes down in flames, this romantic—hero. Can't—knock the damn thing out of my head.

> *Pause. Highwayman music rising. Olivia recites softly to herself.*

Olivia: "He did not come in the dawning. He did not come at noon."

Manon: David?

Olivia: "And out of the tawny sunset, before the rise of the moon."

> *Olivia senses a presence. Jemmy appears behind her. Manon holds David.*

Manon: Oh, you're shaking, David. I'm right here.

> *They kiss.*

Jemmy: *(To Olivia.)* "A red-coat troop came marching—
Marching, marching—
King George's men came marching,
   up to the old inn-door."

> *Manon and David kiss again, suddenly urgent. Olivia can't see Jemmy, doesn't turn to look for him, but knows he's there.*

Olivia: Who are you? What do you want?

> *Drums beat in military fashion as segue into next scene.*

Scene 12

> *The next day, at Olivia's. Erin has been studying. She*
> *sees the envelope with the cash in it on Olivia's desk. She*
> *riffles it, looks around, and puts it back down. Jemmy*
> *startles her. He is in the room with her.*

Jemmy: 'Fink you can turn me into your lapdog, make me be'ave
          nice—don't ya?

Erin: What are you doing here? Stop following me!

Jemmy: If you give me little treats, make me 'fink y'er fallin' for
          me, then maybe you can 'andle me, ain't that right?

Erin: Stay away from me, Jemmy. I don't want to see you
          anymore.

Jemmy: Yeah, I knows thet doddle—you remind me o' someone,
          'tis comin' clear. 'Twas the day I lost me eye, the reason I
          got this scar.

> *He's energized; he acts it out.*

          A dawn raid, me an' my men, we're waitin' in this grove,
          mornin' mist. Mail coach rolls along, filled wiv
          merchants an' money, an' one little lady all in forest
          green. We bring 'em down just afore a stretch o' woods.
          The lady steps out lively when we ask 'er, she's right
          scared, but I sees that an' tells 'er, "I'd never 'arm an 'air
          of yer 'ead. It's jus' the money we're after." And I kiss 'er
          'and. Me men do too, all o' 'em. An' when we rides off, I
          swear, there's tears in 'er eyes. Aaah. It's a mystery.
          Love's a beautiful 'fing, ain't it?

Erin: ...How'd you lose your eye?

Jemmy: *(Beat.)* 'Nother day.

Erin: That's not what really happened, is it?

> *Jemmy picks up the envelope with money in it.*

Jemmy: I seen ya. Wantin' it. Picturin' what you'd spend it on. Y'er not so innocent.

Erin: I know I'm not. I know that.

Jemmy: You ever steal?

Erin: Sometimes.

Jemmy: It made yer 'eart race, I bet, an' you liked that.

Erin: I—did it because I could... And no one ever—caught me.

Jemmy: (Laughs.) Ha! Y'er no better'n me. Stealing's just survival, Erin, showin' 'em yer teeth.

> *He puts his hand around her arm suddenly. She winces; it hurts.*

Ooops, lookie there. Little red mouth pops open again. Shame. What do ya fink it could be sayin'?

> *Erin pulls her arm away. He gestures at the envelope.*

'At's a fair bit o' cash to leave lyin' about. Take it. She's an old lady. She won't miss it. You can tell 'er she's mistaken. That she forgot where she's put it.

Erin: I can't.

Jemmy: "Take it!" says the red lips.

Erin: I don't want to. And I won't cut myself again; you can't make me!

> *He grabs her by the hair; she cries out, shocked and frightened.*

Owww! Let go. You're hurting me.

> *She pulls her pills out of her pocket. In trying to get the lid off, the pills go flying.*

Jemmy: Listen to me, jade. 'Fink you're so smart. 'Fink you can
        get away from me?

        She lashes out and cuffs him.

        Goddammit!

        His nose bleeds. He is angry, then pleased.

        A firebrand, ain't ya?

        *Erin is fighting a rising feeling of approaching
        seizure.*

Erin: I'm stronger than you think. I'm going to fight you.

Jemmy: You can't keep me away.

Erin: I can! I don't want you anymore! Get away from Nan's
        house!

        The highwayman music rising.

Jemmy: 'Member yer vision? When we was ridin' down the
        road? Moon be'ind a cloud, purple sky—sound of 'ooves
        'itting the ground—I just about 'ad ya. You were just
        about there.

Erin: No!

Jemmy: Take that money like I tells ya to, or I'll stuff it down yer
        throat an' choke ya wiv it—an' that's a promise!

        *Lights like the flickering of sunlight through trees from
        a speeding car, then the sound of Erin's sudden seizure
        yell as the lights go to black.*

Scene 13

        *The young woman's voice sings to the beat of a rising
        rhythm.*

Voice: *(Sings.)* "But they gagged his daughter and bound her
                 to the foot of her narrow bed.
            Two of them knelt at the casement,
                 with muskets at their side,
            There was death at every window,
            And hell at one dark window,
            For Bess could see, through her casement,
                 the road that he would ride."

The next night, at Olivia's.

Olivia: How are you feeling?

Erin: Fine. I'm sorry you had to see. I know it's disgusting.

Olivia: It's not. It's going to settle down again, Erin, once your
           system adjusts—

Erin: I know, take my pills like a good girl... Don't worry, I'm
           back in my prison cell, wrapped in plastic. Soon I won't
           feel a thing. I *hope* I won't feel a thing.

Olivia: Erin... We were doing so well. You've—closed down
           suddenly. I feel very inadequate. Talk to me, dear.

Erin: I'm just—*(She clams up.)* No. Nothing.

Olivia: I remember being your age. I was a very different person,
           but I do recall the—I wanted to grow up so desperately,
           but I was so frightened, too.

Erin: I'm not frightened.

Olivia: 'Course you're not. *(Beat.)* Have you heard back from the
           universities?

Erin: Have to get through exams first.

Olivia: Where do you want to go?

Erin: Anywhere. Away.

Olivia: Yes. Do you know what you want to do?

Erin: You mean, what *can* I do.

Olivia: I mean what I said. That was my mistake. I thought
            small, I was frightened and thought small. I went from
            my father's house to my husband's house. Do you know,
            this is the first time in my whole life that I've lived on my
            own?

Erin: *(This registers.)* Really?

Olivia: Yes. At first, when your grandfather died, I was
            terrified—again the fear... All the night noises suddenly
            enormous; I couldn't sleep, didn't want to eat. We're
            both, in our own way, embarked on the same journey,
            you and I—only I'm doing it so much later. So I'd like to
            share it, does that make sense to you? When you called
            me, I was so excited to think we'd be spending time
            together. I wanted to...oh... *(Smiles.)* Isn't this strange? I
            feel—shy. I can't recall feeling shy in—years. But... I've
            been waiting for a grown-up girl in the family, to talk to.
            Share what I know, what you know—

Erin: I don't know anything.

Olivia: You do. If you could just get outside of yourself for a few
            minutes, you'd see.

Erin: No. I'd see horrible things. I *do* see them. I'm a terrible
            person.

Olivia: You're not.

Erin: I have this core of—blackness. Inside. Right here. This
            evil.

            She hits herself. It shocks and worries Olivia.

Olivia: Erin... This is rather difficult. Best just to say it. I'm
            saying it because I want to help, and I want you to know
            that.

            Pause. Olivia gets to her feet.

I think you're allowing yourself to be—self-indulgent. Can you see that, at all?

Erin freezes.

All right. I'll put it another way. When you came here when you were little, you used to take things—books of poetry, small ceramics. I overlooked it; you had enough troubles. I think that's what we all thought, your mother, David, me. Well. Now I'm missing money. Quite a lot. From my desk. Did you take it?

Erin: Did I—?

Olivia: I won't blame you, all right? But I want it back. It's time you stopped. It's time you knew that doing that is wrong.

Erin: I didn't take—

Olivia: Erin, all of us have sorrows, things we think we can't do, pieces of ourselves we're not completely fond of. But we rise above them—you must do that—and you have to start now. You have to get on with your life.

Erin is white, as if she's been slapped.

Erin: I didn't take your money, Nan! How could you think I—

Olivia: Because I've seen you do it. You don't seem to realize you're almost an adult. That you are responsible. I'm sorry if you think I'm being cruel.

Erin: I can't believe that's what you think of me!

She turns away. Silence.

Olivia: You stop yourself, don't you? Won't take the risk. Does that sound hopelessly patronizing? I so don't mean it to be.

She looks at Erin, locked in gloom.

If you could only realize, you and your father. I'm not trying to pry or be nosy. I just want to know. I just simply—care. The hardest thing, Erin? May be having no way of knowing how everything's going to turn out for the people you love. *(Beat.)* What do you want from your life? Maybe you have no idea, or maybe you do but it's just impossible for you to tell me, for any number of reasons... I want you to promise me something. Even if you decide never to admit it to me or to anyone—if you decide to keep that money? I want you to use it to begin your new life. I want you to use it for rent. Or food. Because you're hungry. Because you need it. Because you're doing something that you've thought about doing but hadn't yet had the gumption to do. And see what happens, see what comes next. Embark, for heaven's sake!

> *Beat. Erin pulls the envelope with money out of her pocket and hands it to Olivia. Pause. Olivia pushes it back into Erin's hand.*

You're not baggage anymore, don't you understand? You're the traveller.

> *Sound of David entering, calling.*

David: Mum, Erin, I'm here!

> *Olivia pushes Erin's hand again. Erin puts the money back in her pocket. David has come in, and kisses both.*

Brought you something. Both of you.

> *He hands them a Yellowknife airport bag. Olivia's holds an owl in an Inuit parka, and Erin's a polar bear.*

Erin: Dad...

Olivia: Lovely, dear. You shouldn't have.

David: Steve was in town—he'd been up to Yellowknife, I asked him to— We've been having a terrible time with these two accounts but—hopefully, hopefully...

Erin: Did he see any?

David: Huh?

          Erin waves the polar bear at him. He flops onto the couch.

          No idea. I'm exhausted.

Olivia: David? I'm so glad you're here. Is it all right if Erin goes home with you?

          Erin looks at Olivia, surprised.

David: Of course! Great.

Olivia: It's been wonderful, but—I haven't told you this yet, Erin, I'm so sorry—I'd planned a little trip that I'd almost forgotten, and—well, I've realized I won't be able to drive you in for that last exam. You don't mind, dear, do you?

Erin: No… I'll—get packed then.

          Erin gets up and exits. Olivia watches her go.

David: Has she been—?

Olivia: There was a seizure, yesterday. She's ashamed, I think. We—lost some of the ground we'd gained. But we've survived. It's been good.

David: I'm glad.

          He prowls around, looking at things, rather like Jemmy does.

Olivia: Did you—have a chance to look into my stocks and things? I know you've been busy, but—

David: Actually, I did do some checking.

Olivia: Oh, yes. And?

David: Well, you've got a fair amount, all pretty standard stuff.

Olivia: Your father put them into safer areas, when he was ill.

David: Thing is, you could do a lot better, if you upped the stakes, got into something that's climbing. Some things are doing phenomenally, Mum.

Olivia: I haven't needed to touch it.

David: Your money's losing ground, I just hate to see it. It's totally up to you, of course. But that's what I found out.

Olivia: I have enough, that's the point. It's what my lawyer's assured me. However. After I talked with the people at the bank, I met with him, and—because I know so little—and care so little—about the making of money, I thought—well, I decided to sign over power of attorney of the stocks—to you.

David: Mum... I'm—flabbergasted.

Olivia: *(Deliberately.)* So. It's up to you. See what you can do.

David: Mum—thanks, I'll—I'm sure I can make it turn a much better profit—

Olivia: We can talk about it later. Go and get some sleep.

> *Erin has entered with her bags. David takes them from her, looks at Olivia again, and exits.*

Erin: Nan?

Olivia: Yes?

Erin: You don't hate me, do you?

Olivia: Oh, my darling. Absolutely the opposite.

Erin: But I *should* go, I think. I have this bad feeling, like if I stay—

Olivia: What, dear?

Erin: I don't want anything bad to happen here.

Olivia: Neither do I. *(Quietly.)* It takes time and it's painful. But worth it. All right? Go on, dear. You'll be fine.

> *Olivia kisses Erin and Erin goes. Jemmy appears. Olivia, sensing him, is very still.*

(Recites.) "The tip of one finger touched it.
She strove no more for the rest.
Up, she stood up to attention,
   with the muzzle beneath her breast—
She would not risk their hearing;
   she would not strive again "

Jemmy: *(Recites.)* "For the road lay bare in the moonlight;
Blank and bare in the moonlight;"

Jemmy & Olivia: *(Together.)* "And the blood of her veins, in the moonlight,
   throbbed to her love's refrain."

> *Pause.*

Olivia: Don't go. Stay with me.

Scene 14

> *Several days later. David, in his office, making a call.*

David: David Dafoe. Have you got that breakdown for me? Listen, it's got to be a fast turnover, that's the whole point. To the best of your knowledge... I know you have to warn me, but I've been watching the... Commodities. Yeah, and? Diversify, sure, a little bit, but— 'Course I know the risk. You're sweating? Hey, it's my money. No, that sounds good, yeah. Move them there.

> *He disconnects, then speed dials again on his cellphone.*

Steve. It's David. I've found a way. *(Grins.)* Of course I'm worried. When am I not? Never mind how. Yeah, so we need how much by...? *(Looks at a calendar.)* Yeah, I can do it. No, things are evening out here. I'm hoping I'll be able

to pull up stakes by—September? Once Erin's settled.
You were thinking…? Manon? You think so? Sure, it's a
good idea. I'm behind it. We'll need to find another
office—more money. *(Laughs.)* One of us should be in
real estate, the rate we're going. Get working on it, will
you? Yeah.

> *He hangs up. Suddenly he pauses, looks haunted. Then
> he calls out.*

Manon? You there?

> *She enters, with a coffee.*

Manon: What's up?

David: Before Steve calls, I want to tell you myself. It's
confidential, and everything's up in the air still but—the
branch office here? We may be going for it. We'd like you
to head it up if we do.

Manon: What? Whoa! That's fantastic! We're doing all right
then?

David: We're doing business.

Manon: I'm so happy for you guys—for us! Hell, for me!

> *She hugs him so hard David nearly falls over. Erin
> enters in the middle of it. She stops, looks at them both.*

David: Hon. Hi.

Erin: Hi.

Manon: How was the exam?

Erin: Horrible. But it was the last one.

> *Beat. Erin goes up to Manon.*

Manon? I'm sorry about what I said to you, that time. It
was very rude.

Manon: That's ok. I—

Erin: Let me start again?

>*She holds out her hand. Manon looks at it, then takes it.*

I apologize for being a little creep.

Manon: Oh, well... That's ok, not a problem.

Erin: Dad's pretty revved these days. I think you've cheered him up.

David: Actually, that's true. Along with another bit of news. Geoterme's on the up, Air. Manon's going to run a branch here, and—we're moving to Calgary. Looks like. What do you say?

Erin: Now?

David: Well, soon, yeah. Put the house on the—

Erin: The thing is—Dad? I want to get my own place.

David: What?

Erin: Something small, like with students, or shared, I don't care. But I need a job, and—

David: Erin, you're—

Erin: I just want to—think, somewhere, on my own, this summer. Before I have to decide anything. I just want to do it. On my own.

David: I'm not sure this is the right time to—

Erin: Yes, it is. You want to go to Calgary, sell our house. You're changing. So can I. I want to. I won't come with you.

David: Where did this idea come from?

Erin: From me.

David: Where you going to get the money?

Erin: I hoped—you could help. To start with. And then—a job.
           I don't need much.

Manon: I did that, moved out. It was great. Best thing I'd ever
           done.

David: Manon…

Manon: Well, it was.

Erin: What did you do?

           David gives Manon a look; she looks back at Erin.

Manon: I was eighteen. I moved in with my cousin, at university.
           She had a place with four others. It was—wonderful. I
           lay on the grass in the backyard, on my back, and did
           nothing, all summer.

David: You're not helping.

Manon: Well, that's what happened. I made all the decisions I've
           been happy about since. *(Laughs.)* It wasn't till later that I
           got confused again.

Erin: Come on, Dad. You're doing what you want to do.

David: Have you thought what living with other people will be
           like, if you don't know them and you have a… Or if
           you're on your own? Nobody around? I'd be calling
           every few minutes.

Erin: So don't! I won't answer!

           She storms into her room.

David: Erin! …Acch! Why'd she bring this up now? With you
           here?

Manon: I thought it was pretty shrewd, myself…

David: Don't interfere when it comes to my daughter, Manon.
           All right?

Manon: Whoa. I'm not interfering. I was asked my opinion.

David: Damn!

Manon: I can't believe you…said that.

David: Ok, I'm not handling this very well, I recognize. I didn't mean to come at you like that. But. You have to know, if we're to continue?—how can I put it?

Manon: I don't know. Carefully, I hope.

David: Erin and I are already a team. We work together in a certain way—

Manon: Yes? And?

David: I need you to respect that, to—

Manon: I do.

David: Erin isn't the one that has to fit in—it's you. Do you see what I mean, at all? Or—am I putting this badly?

Manon: You—must be putting it badly. But I get the gist. Maybe I should leave you to—sort this out?

David: Sorry, Manon, sorry… I've got too much on my mind…

Manon: No, no. Don't sweat it. What do I know about kids, right? It's just that—well. I do remember *being* one. Maybe since I've never been in there, duking it out, on the other side. Never mind.

Scene 15

> *Olivia's house. Jemmy is behind Olivia (possibly scrimmed), but it is as if she sees him in front of her, and they are talking together.*

Olivia: You've a fine baritone. Do you know this one? *(Sings.)* "Bold and yet undaunted—"

Jemmy: *(Sings.)* "—was young Brennan on the moor." Cor, yeah. Know 'em all. I likes the ballads. You sing 'em good.

Olivia: Once, when I was a girl, not much younger than my granddaughter, I had a pony. It was a wild little thing, very shaggy. Mostly white, with brown patches, and one pale blue eye. It had been treated badly, I think, and it nipped.

Jemmy: What's thet to me, then?

Olivia: None of my friends could ride it. It would buck them off and I'd feel so terrible. We tried everything. Then one day, I—

> *She stands, holds out her arms.*

Jemmy: What you up to?

Olivia: Steady.

> *As if he is there, she takes him by the "ears" and breathes into his nose. He "breathes" it in, then sneezes.*

Jemmy: Why'd you do thet?

> *Olivia sits again, laughing, but in pain. Jemmy rubs his nose.*

Olivia: And you a horseman with a love for your steed? *(Beat.)* I've been glad of your company these past days.

Jemmy: Eh, well, ya never knows what can 'appen, eh?

> *Lights also on David's office. The phone rings. David has been poised, waiting for it. During the call, Erin enters and hears it. Jemmy turns to look at David.*

David: David Dafoe. What's happening? No! When did that—? How much did I lose? Jesus Christ, I know, but—? What else is dropping? You're kidding! So your advice is? A correction in the— Yeah, yeah, you schmuck!—I know you told me. I'm not some idiot! I know! Just—watch it like a hawk, would ya, just—earn your money for once!

He disconnects, and stares into space. Jemmy watches Erin.

Erin: Dad? You're in trouble, aren't you?

David: Huh? No, I'm not in trouble. Maybe a bit—preoccupied.

Erin: I'm so worried about you—

David: What are you worried about *me* for, hey?

Erin: It's scaring me, Dad—

David: Oh, sweetie, it's ok…

David hugs Erin.

Olivia: Promise me.

Jemmy: *(Looks at Olivia.)* Can't promise nuffin'.

Olivia: I'll have to rely on your being a gentleman, then.

Jemmy: *(Laughs.)* When 'ell freezes over! *(Looks back at Erin.)*

David: I'm sorry I jumped on your idea.

Erin: It's not that!

David: It surprised me, that's all. And your mother might not be able to help. She's—

Erin: Dad, don't. *Don't.*

Olivia: *(To Jemmy.)* I think you underestimate yourself.

Erin: I know you and Mum aren't getting back together. I'm sorry for the way I was about Manon—

David: Couple of things are making me—jumpy, Erin, but once the Yellowknife deal goes through—

Erin: You always say that. Once this, and then once that. It's always just about to happen. It's never "then." It's never over. I need it to be over, Dad.

David holds Erin. He is fighting his own panic.

David: Tell you what. We'll travel somewhere this summer, some European spa town, just like your grandmother, eh?

Erin: That'd be—nice.

Jemmy: *(To Olivia.)* You ain't afraid o' me, are ya?

Olivia: Oh yes, I am. But I never expected you'd be so—beguiling.

David strokes Erin's hair.

David: We're going to be fine.

Jemmy: Does it hurt?

Olivia: Yes. It does.

David: Everything's going to turn around for us.

Jemmy: "Tlot-tlot, had they heard it?
         The horse hooves ringing clear;
         Tlot-tlot, in the distance?
         Were they deaf that they did not hear?"

         As Jemmy continues, David's cellphone rings. He can't help himself; he answers, and Erin turns away. Lights fade on them.

David: *(Into phone.)* David Dafoe.

         Jemmy moves down and into Olivia's room.

Jemmy: "Down the ribbon of moonlight,
            over the brow of the hill—
         The highwayman came riding—
         Riding—riding—"

Olivia: "The red-coats looked to their priming!
         She stood up, straight and still."

Jemmy is now directly behind Olivia's chair.

Jemmy: I'd never 'arm an 'air o' yer 'ead. Ya know thet, don't ya?

Scene 16

Sound of horses' hooves, galloping, coming closer. There is more than one horse, there are cries and shots in the air, sounds of "whoa!" Erin's bedroom. Middle of that night. She is dreaming, thrashing in her bed.

Erin: He's... No! Let me...out. I can't—breathe!

She wakes up, looks around, dazed. Jemmy appears in her room, in his full regalia.

Jemmy...?

Jemmy: Mail coach was late today. Was you scared, milady— tearin' along, wiv us in pursuit? It's a thrill, but it's good to finally stop, don't you 'fink? Step down, now. Don't be afeared.

Erin is frightened; this "Jemmy reality" is different. Sounds of unseen men, horses stamping—the sounds of the dawn robbery. Through the following, it is as if it's happening all around her, as if she can also see the other "men."

Erin: Who's—? What's happening...

Jemmy: At's it. Lovely laidy, all in green.

He turns as if speaking to his men.

Keep the gentlemen back there, lads. Just reach in and 'ave their wallets and pocketwatches—don't forget the rings. 'At's a nice one that, thank ye, sir. *(To Erin.)* Come along, me pretty. I won't 'arm ya. Just need a little kiss, in the mornin' light. Ain't you the lucky one.

As he kisses her, she takes his knife and hides it behind her back. He doesn't notice. She pulls away.

Now, now. You've 'eard o' me. Capt'n Thunderball. I'm famous all along this stretch o' highway. Bein' robbed by me's the thrill o' yer lifetime.

He moves towards her again.

I wouldn't 'arm an 'air o' yer 'ead. *(Whispered, conspiratorial.)* Relax now. Nearly there.

With a swift movement, Erin stabs him in the eye. He roars with pain and falls back.

Bitch! Vile, filthy—bitch! Lads! Me eye, goddammit— she's put out me eye! Piss off, codgers. Whip up the coach! If you value your lives, get out o' 'ere! Leave 'er with us! Go!

Sounds of whips cracking, men yelling, horses and coach moving off at a gallop. Jemmy, streaming blood, comes towards Erin.

You shouldn't'a put up such a fight, milady. It's goin' to be so much more painful now.

Erin: No!

As Jemmy reaches for her, she stabs him again. The sky explodes in purple—a big face, Olivia's, flashes in the purple sky, the bedroom disappearing; the words at the end of the verse need to be very clearly heard.

Voice: *(Sings.)* "Her eyes grew wide for a moment;
               she drew one last deep breath,
           Then her finger moved in the moonlight,
           Her musket shattered the moonlight,
           Shattered her breast in the moonlight,
               and warned him—with her death."

The seizure ends and Erin lies, alone, on her bedroom floor. She realizes.

Erin: …Nan. Oh, no, it's Nan!

             Shakily, she gets to her feet and goes downstairs. David
             has fallen asleep in front of his computer screen.

             Dad, wake up!

David: Erin?—Air, what's wrong?

             Erin goes off, for her shoes and the car keys.

Erin: We have to go, right now!

David: Did you—have a seizure, what—?

Erin: Hurry!

David: I don't understand—

             Erin enters again, gives the keys to David.

Erin: There's no time! We have to go to Nan's—come on!

David: You've had a nightmare. Is that what happened? I'll get
             you some water, ok?

Erin: No!

             He puts the keys down.

David: We'll call her. Make sure she's all right. Just—stay there.

             Erin sits. He exits to the kitchen. She jumps up, takes the
             keys, and exits running. He re-enters with water.

             Erin? Oh, no.

             He runs out after her.

             Erin!

             He re-enters, dials Olivia's number.

             Come on, Mum—come on!

Olivia, in her house, hears the phone ring. She tries to answer it, but falls and lies still. David has his cellphone at his other ear.

(*Into cellphone.*) Manon? It's David. Erin's taken the car. She's headed to my mother's. I think she had a seizure or— How soon can you get here? Thanks—hurry!

Scene 17

Crossfade to Olivia's house. It is very dark. Erin enters.

Erin: Nan? Where are you?

           She turns on a lamp. She sees her grandmother on the floor.

Erin: Nan? How did you get—? I knew. I saw you. I—

           Olivia is very weak.

Olivia: The phone rang. I thought—it must be an emergency…

Erin: I can hardly hear you—

Olivia: Erin? You mustn't… Darling? I don't want to fight it anymore.

Erin: I have to call an ambulance—I—

Olivia: I've tried to think of everything… I just want to go. I'm very tired.

           She dies.

Erin: Oh… No, no…! Nan?

           David and Manon enter. The following dialogue, until Erin hangs up the phone, should overlap as it would in such a situation.

David: Erin, where's your—? Oh, no.

Erin: She's—

David: Mum. Did you know she was this ill? Why didn't I
            know?

Erin: I—didn't know either.

            David falls to his knees beside his mother.

David: Mum… Please, Mum. *(To Olivia, holding her body.)* I made
            a mistake, Mum. All your stocks. They warned me—I've
            been watching the market all year—it's been rocketing.
            Now it's—sliding, it's falling—and Steve, the business—
            It's killing me, Mum. I don't know what to do… I don't
            know what to do now…

Manon: Did you find her here?

            Erin nods, watching David.

            We should call an ambulance. *(On her cellphone.)* I need
            an ambulance.

Erin: I know the address. *(She takes the phone.)* 1421 Everdon.
            The second road to the right. Hurry? *(Hangs up.)*

Manon: David? Dave?

            *Manon reaches out to comfort David, who hunches
            protectively over his mother's body.*

David: Get away from me! Don't you understand anything!

            Erin and Manon are scared, shocked.

Erin: Dad… Please. Let go of her.

            Erin hugs David; he tries to shake her off.

Manon: I think I'll—they might miss the road if—

            Manon slips out.

Erin: Dad. It's peace she wants. No, Dad!

> *David is grieving and dangerous—Erin clings on, as the lights fade on them. Jemmy, in moonlight, as at the beginning of the play, animated, roaring—speaking or singing his own demise.*

Jemmy: "Back he spurred like a madman,
               shrieking a curse to the sky,
          With the white road smoking behind him,
               and his rapier brandished high!
          Blood-red were his spurs i' the golden noon;
               wine-red was his velvet coat;
          When they shot him down on the highway,
          Down like a dog on the highway,
          And he lay in his blood on the highway,
               with a bunch of lace at his throat."

Scene 18

> *One month later. Lights up on "office" during voiceover, as David enters with a computer box. He puts it down and begins dismantling equipment.*

Voiceover: *(Three voices)* ...The country's biggest bank triggered a stampede out of bank stocks yesterday when it warned that its third-quarter profit will be well below expectations... The hearing tomorrow into allegations that there were misrepresentations of involvement in mutual fund trading... High fliers in the computer industry have been losing altitude since the recent bout of market volatility has dropped their stock prices...

> *Manon enters, hesitant. David sees her and pauses.*

Manon: I just let myself in. I hope that's all right.

David: 'Course. There's a box in the hall, did you see it? Most of the pertinent files are there. I'll be shipping everything else tomorrow, so if there's anything you want to add—

Manon: Did you get the ones from my desk?

David: Yeah. (Re: the furniture.) This is all going back tomorrow, too.

Manon: *(Beat.)* I'm sorry, Dave. Your mother—

> *He stops her.*

> The business—

David: I *wanted* to sell. Steve already had this guy in *mind*, it turns out. He wanted in, I wanted out. New partners. Piece of cake.

Manon: You were right. Steve *is* ruthless, I know that. *(Beat.)* I may not stay. There's new firms opening up in Vancouver. But I need to find out whether this what I really want. You understand that, don't you?

David: Watch your back.

> *She nods. He goes back to what he is doing.*

Manon: Well. If there's nothing else…

> *She turns to go.*

David: I thought my mother didn't know. That I'd been reckless with the stocks. But she did. She knew exactly.

Manon: What do you mean?

> *Erin enters, carrying a knapsack and her computer case.*

Erin: Oh, hi. I didn't know you were here.

Manon: Well, I'm just going.

Erin: Manon? I wanted to tell you— I'm going to spend some time in the grass, thinking.

Manon: *(To Erin, warmly.)* Good. *(To David.)* That's really good.

Erin: And I'm on a new drug, doesn't flatten everything out so
          much. Sometimes still shitty, but. *(Beat.)* Thanks for your
          help. We really appreciated it.

Manon: I wish I could have done more.

          She and Erin kiss. Then, to David:

          Take care.

          Manon exits. Erin watches David for a moment.

Erin: Dad?

David: Ready, then?

Erin: Yeah.

David: Got your keys?

          Erin nods.

          Don't forget to lock up at night. It's an old house. It's
          isolated.

Erin: Dad, I'll be fine.

          She pulls a letter out of her knapsack.

          I want to open this now. Can you—?

David: It's for you.

Erin: I know, but.

          David opens it, reads.

David: "Erin. You may wonder what a girl your age has to do
          with the owning of a house, and you may feel it's the
          worst burden anyone could have inflicted on you. If you
          feel that way, sell it. Make sure you get a good price for it,
          but sell it. If you have any doubts—wait a while. I have
          great expectations for your future. And for your father's,
          too. Nan."

Erin: Sure you won't come with me?

David: I've got to—sort a bunch of stuff out, Air.

Erin: *(She nods.)* Like the ballad says: she warned us, with her death. Because she loved us.

> *Erin hugs him, then exits. David looks around the office. The phone rings. He pauses, then ignores it, goes on packing. The phone goes on into the blackout.*
>
> *Sound of hooves, galloping closer, and a horse's laboured breathing, rising to a final crescendo. Jemmy appears, in silhouette—looks over at David. Just as David senses his presence there—swift blackout.*
>
> *As curtain descends, the young woman's voice singing final verse of poem can be heard.*

Voice: "And still of a winter's night, they say,
            when the wind is in the trees,
          When the moon is a ghostly galleon
            tossed upon cloudy seas,"
          When the road is a ribbon of moonlight
            over the purple moor,
          A highwayman comes riding—
            Riding—riding—
          A highwayman comes riding, up to the old inn-door."

    END

HUNGER STRIKING

For Anna Elmberg Wright, and Ella

"All women are not always lovely,
and the wild women never are."
　　　　　　　—Lady Eliza Lynn Linton (1891)

Binnorie
(traditional)

freely

What did you want, lass,　in the dark wood?　Did you

come to pick ber-ries or dream that you could

find your heart's desire there, well, you'd　better stayed a–way, for the

bright lads of sum — mer　ne-ver　came　that　way.

Production Credits

Hunger Striking was first produced by Theatre Passe Muraille in Toronto, Ontario, in 1998.

Directed by Janet Amos
Production Design by Ana Cappelluto
Original Music and Sound Design by Cathy Nosaty
Stage Managed by Christine Oakey

CAST
Catherine McNally as Sarah

Hunger Striking owes many things to many people, for sharing stories and images, as well as laughs and tears. Thanks especially to Andrew Willmer, for always being...you know. To my mother, Beth, with much love. To Janet, Ana, Cathy, Christine and Catherine, to Layne Coleman and the entire staff at Passe Muraille. To Sharon Pollock, Kelley Jo Burke, Peter Smith, Lise Ann Johnson, Diana Fajrajsl, Maggie Nagle, and my Writer's Unit buddies at Playwrights' Workshop Montreal, to Julia Dover, Wolfgang Vachon, Bonnie Harnden, Octavia James, Evalyn Parry, Rebecca Doll, and to Concordia University for a generous Faculty Research Development Grant.

Director's Notes

During my second incarnation as Artistic Director of the Blyth Festival, I had come across two plays by Kit Brennan, *Spring Planting* and *Magpie*. In 1996, while working in Montreal, I was able, finally, to make her acquaintance and she gave me two more. *Tiger's Heart* was a fascinating play inspired by the life of Dr. James Barry, a nineteenth century woman who, disguised as a man, had an extraordinary career as a military doctor. The second was a new play called *Hunger Striking*, based on Kit's own experience with anorexia.

At the time, I had only the vaguest notions about anorexia and its causes. Reading *Hunger Striking* I was able, for the first time, to understand the terrible grip of this condition. I was overwhelmed, not only by the detailed description of how and why anorexia occurs, but by the powerful imaginative context of Sarah's journey. The recurring Irish imagery pulls us into ever-deeper psychological levels and allows the documentary form to draw on myth.

We are also pulled into Sarah's mind, into "that warped anorexic logic" which seeks power through self-control and redemption through self-destruction. At first, all of Sarah's goals appear compelling and reasonable. She is powerful, sardonic and heroic, and bears, as it were, the sins and guilt of our times. By the end, she finds herself almost consumed by a desperate struggle not only to save her wasted body and loosened mind, but to rediscover, at very great cost, the will to live.

Needless to say, I was very excited by *Hunger Striking*. Grants from the Canada Council and the Ontario Arts Council made possible a workshop and assisted in the production. We were most fortunate in the support of Layne Coleman and his wonderful staff at Theatre Passe Muraille in Toronto.

Many thanks also to our creative production team. Ana Cappelluto's evocative lighting and dynamic use of space transformed The Back Space into a versatile and fluid setting. Cathy Nosaty's soundscape was haunting, spare, and powerful. Catherine McNally as Sarah was wonderful to work with. Her versatility, her emotional commitment, and her daring physicality were an inspiration and a joy to watch.

Finally, I want to thank Kit Brennan. *Hunger Striking* is not just a play about anorexia. It is a story of resilience, survival, and rebirth. It brings light and courage to our world.

—Janet Amos

Staging Notes

Casting Requirements
> Sarah, a woman between 33 and 45 years of age.

Setting
> An outdoor space.

Notes

Hunger Striking takes place during one afternoon or evening. During this time, Sarah travels from the here and now—her reality as a teacher of high school English—into her own past, via Irish mythology, and the suffragettes at the turn of the last century.

Survivors of painful events never lose their sense of humour—it is one of the elements which saves them. For those who wish to perform or produce the play, the kind of dark, wild humour that runs throughout is a crucial part of the fabric of the experience. Also, for those seeking an understanding of Sarah's quick switches of behaviour in the depths of her illness, a key lies in the line: "They hear voices, sit still for hours at a time or *explode* screaming and running." Sarah's rebellion is changeling-like, sly. She pits her wits against the doctors', outwitting and outsmarting the plebs all around her, with an energy and spirit that keeps her moving forward. Connected with that is her love and desire to follow her father's Celtic roots, to be his boy. There must never be a heaviness or any sense of self pity—the heightened state to which one arrives when deprived of food tends to make the cosmos and everything that is happening appear to be an adventure that one must win, rather than a place where one needs therapy and self-analysis. It also seems more useful to celebrate strength and resiliency, the ability humans have to turn things around. Anorexia is a struggle between brain and body even more than mind and spirit, seductive and deadly, but not impossible to outwit. And it's a battle worth winning.

The play is in one act, of approximately 90 minutes. There is no intermission.

Hunger Striking

An outdoor space. Sarah is discovered in it.

Sarah:
Do you know about changelings? For some reason, the babies of fairies—of the little people, who live in Tir na n'Og, the land of eternal youth—their babies are born old before their time and wizened and mean—while the babies of humans—

She stops, hesitates.

…the babies of humans…are born—plump and rosy and…happy. *(Pause.)* So…the fairies exchange them, in the dead of night. The mother fairy puts her baby in the crib and steals the human one—takes it back to Tir na n'Og. And the changeling, in the morning, is there in the crib, ugly, horrible, and the human family is left to bring it up. But it's never healthy. You can look in its eyes and there's nothing human there.

Pause.

I tried to talk to her, I tried to get through. All right, I feel guilty, I feel terrible!

I can't stay. I can't go on. The whole school's in a mess—everyone in shock, huddles of girls in the halls, crying. It feels, somehow—I'm sorry, but honestly—cheap and sentimental. I—

Forget it. Not worth it. No.

Your mother. Your own mother, Katie. We're standing there, at your graveside, and she says to me, she says, "If only I'd taken the mirror out of her room. If only I could have kept her away from the magazines and the television, all the media glamour. If only she could have had a boyfriend." And she's sobbing and grasping at the only kinds of answers she can understand, and rage grabs me by the throat and I want to fling her into the grave after you. How can they begin to understand when—? Christ.

And now, this morning. I've been feeling strange, right? I put it down to your death and the way it happened. I go to my doctor. I want some nausea capsules. Think it will take ten minutes. She comes out with a huge smile on her face. I find out I'm pregnant! I get in the car. I am stunned. It is the biggest cosmic joke I have ever— I drive. It all falls into place. I am full of strange hormones. It's foreign and frightening. It's like going back, going there. Being out of control, taken over. Some kind of alien force. If you don't feed this little fish, it will eat the calcium in your teeth, the shine in your hair. This is not a fashionable feeling. I will be made to pay for this one.

No, no, little fish, this is stony ground. You will not thrive here. Go back.

There's a belief in Ireland, in Tir na n'Og—the land of eternal youth. Once you get there, if you get there, there's no coming back. There's several ways to go, none of them foolproof. You can ride a kelpie, you can cross over by crawling through a stone, you can be chosen—but if you try to come back, and any part of your physical body touches the earth, you will shrivel into a pile of dust on the spot. I grew up believing in things like this. It explained a lot.

This is solving nothing. Make that call, go to work—make life simple and go on. No. Think what I really think for once, silence be damned—

I cannot, I will not, bring a girl into this world.

There.

Yes, I'm a feminist. No, I'm not sexist. I try not to be. I also try not to label people with "ists." Yes, I'm a good teacher; they tell me what an influence I've had, and yes, I take their problems home with me sometimes. This time. That's not—professional? Thank you. I quit! You'll have my letter in the morning!

…One day, late fall, the school washroom. I'd just noticed that maybe, just maybe, Katie was losing weight. Her clothes were baggier. She was changing her style to hide the fact. I was in a cubicle, peering through the crack. There was that something about her, the intensity, the loathing—I watched her watch herself. It was like…overhearing a man beating his wife through the wall of a semi… Her eye and the mirror. Strip search, slow and critical.

She turns towards me, and there's no distance—I am her. Everything is me. I am everything I see.

Katie.

"Oh! Ms. O'Brien, you scared me. I didn't know anyone was in here."

And it's gone—I'm her teacher again. I scrabble to bury the rubble, hers and mine.

"I didn't mean to scare you. Are you—is there anything I can do?"

"What do you mean? Did I do badly on my test?"

"No. No! I just—you're looking pale. Are you—eating enough?"

How could I say that? How could I have forgotten?

Her face seals. "Oh, yeah, like a horse. I gotta go. Bye, Ms. O'Brien."

She drinks whisky from a flask.

She wrote a story in January. She called it "The Singing Bones."

"There were two sisters. Like sisters anywhere, they shared marrow, and it hurt to do so. They walked one day through fields, up a hill, to the coast. There was a cliff, high high above the sea breaking below. The elder sister, suddenly and without warning, pushed the younger over the edge. The younger went over, turning end over end through the air, hit the water, which was cold and salt. The elder clambered down the cliff edge, hair blowing wildly over her face. The girl in the water reached out: help me? The elder pried her sister's fingers loose from the rocks. This was colder than water. The younger swam like a seal for the centre of the sea.

"The elder scrabbled and hauled herself back up the cliff face. She ran through the fields shrieking, help me help me! There was a grand funeral five days later. Our daughter! Our sweet one! Poor sister, poor darling. An elaborate coffin went into the ground— minus a body.

"The younger sister had battled the sea, tried to be a seal, but hadn't the flippers for it. She drowned, lungs full of salt water. Eventually, the body washed up on shore. Over time, her bones were washed clean on the rocks, and nothing remained but the essentials. Bones, hair, sinew. The breast bone began to sing as the wind whistled through it. A harper came by, and was full of awe. Surely with such an instrument, I might make my fortune! He put it under his arm, and that night came to a castle. Can I sing for my supper? I have a wonderful harp.

"Candlelight, smoky tapers, dogs underfoot and lush tapestries. Lord and lady, and elder daughter. The musician sets the harp upon the table, and loudly it begins to sing, alone, of a walk on a cliff edge, of a sudden—betrayal—and the jealous murder of sister by sister."

She drinks again.

I tell Katie nice things. I mention my own knowledge of different forms of the tale—a mythic archetype, numerous ballads—but I am a typical grade twelve teacher and I do not go into the hard and fast of it. I don't tell her the ballad's connection to my own life. I am silent although I speak at great length—why? I see her eyes watching me…am I following? She is turning back to see if I'm there—and I'm not. I've been put to sleep, I've been gutted while I wasn't looking and I haven't even noticed—I've done it to myself?

Katie's breath. Smelt of death. Burning her own muscles, her body eating itself to stay alive. I check my breath all the time. Still. I try to be surreptitious—carry mints. I recognize others, something in the eyes—leave a bit of food on the plate to prove we still can. No one talks about that, about recovered anorexics. Teeth full of metal, brittle bones—an ovary shrivelled, that's what they told me. I thought I was safe. God! Never safe…

She drinks again.

No, I'm not an alcoholic, I'm Irish-Canadian. I know. That's not funny. Many true things are not funny. Have to drink something every time I eat. Still afraid of my throat closing, the food getting stuck—choking—choking...

How did it start? And how did I do it? How did I turn it around and not end up like you, Katie?

It was a horrible death. In the cafeteria. People screaming. Why were you there? You never ate in front of people...

Your chair scrapes, you stand up, eyes wide. Everyone looks. Choking, a morsel of food, it sticks in your throat—you fall to the floor, jerk once, and are gone. I am there, holding you, I feel the hurricane of your weightless passion, the stench of your breath, pass through me and out, a selkie slipping her animal skin—lighter than air—at last.

She sings.

> What did you want, lass,
> in the dark wood?
> Did you come to pick berries
> or dream that you could
> find your heart's desire there?
> Well, you had better stayed away
> for the bright lads of summer
> never came that way.

She drinks.

My dad was from Kilkenny, Ireland. Big on belief in the Irish gods. I loved him intensely, a dark brooding love. Dad's dad was a butcher, poor, Protestant; fed his family on offal—heart, liver, tongue. Dad sang in a choir till his voice changed; I try to imagine it, skinny little freckled kid in a white cassock, pure as the driven snow but really a hellion, raised on pure protein, racing around with his pals and drinking the sacramental wine. By the time I came along, Dad had had enough of organized anything, and refused to indoctrinate us, as he called it. He was always going on about the Irish gods, how you have to be so careful—they're up there, waiting. If you wake up on Saturday morning and it's a beautiful day, and you say, "great! I *knew* it would be perfect"—a huge cumulus mass will suddenly rear up on the horizon, hunker down directly over your head and dump a ton of water on it. Once I asked, "Dad, how come the gods're over here with us? Don't they have enough people's lives to wreck in Ireland?" He said, "They see all, Sarah. Anyone with a drop of Irish."

He was in his late forties when I was born; I was the bright lad of his darker days. "Dad! Watch this!" In the fields near our house, a scarf in the waistband of my pants, I twist my head and watch it dance, dream of my coming glorious beast life. Kelpie, a mythical creature, inhabits my head. Half-man, half-horse. It lives near marshes, bogs and lowlands, and it bursts out of the water on its way to Tir na n'Og. You leap on its back, go where you can be ever young. Kelpie tears off across the bog. You hang on for dear life, shriek and laugh your joy. All is well as it heads inland, but if it catches a scent of the sea, you'd better pray there'll be someone there at the water's edge to grab onto your heels as it gallops past or you'll be drowned in a flash and without remorse. Hi, Kelpie! "Hello, boy." I am the boy on the kelpie's back, and sometimes I am the kelpie—together we're wild!

(Stops.) It's a horse. I don't want to play with Anne. She's being mean. I like being alone.

Kelpie goes underground. Doesn't sit at the table anymore, doesn't climb snorting into my bed. It's easier to keep quiet than try to explain.

She sits abruptly on the ground.

Why, Daddy? He's crying. I want to.

"He's not our dog."

But *why*!? He's in the dark all the time in the shed!

"No, sweetheart. He has food and shelter. The SPCA says if he has those there's nothing we can do. You have to ignore it."

I won't!

"Sit on my knee, Sarah. Come on, let me tell you a story. Last time I was in Ireland to visit your Gran"—

—the one with the crystal bead necklace?—

"—the very same. Well, on the way back I thought I'd go across the water, before I came home. I'm an old soul, can't keep me away… And do you know where I went?"

No.

"To the standing stones, to Stonehenge."

What's that?

"A place of power. No matter how they rob it of its majesty, Sarah, there's a calm and an eternity always there."

What's an eternity?

"It's a wish to never leave."

And he hugs me hard. Daddies don't cry. I am very still. I think of the dog next door, waiting in the dark for his world to change. Why doesn't he howl? I am scared by the tears in my hair…

She drinks.

Ten to twelve are the golden years for girls. It's before gender, pre-gender. Sort of. Already you're aware that that's a big battlefield. Already the boys know it's one they have to win. And the traitor, the snake in the grass, is your body—it's on their side. *(A wail.)* Muuuuumm, what *is* this? Am I dying, or what?

"Sit down, Sarah, in the bathroom. Here, sit here. You're fine."

I'm dying!

"You're not. This is normal. It happens every month."

…What?

"You'll get used to it."

I'm eleven years old. I'm dying!

"You're maturing early... It's perfectly natural. There's a book you can read."

A book! ...How long does this go on?

"About a week every month."

For how long!

"Forever. Till you're old and you die."

No doubt I hear wrong. No doubt she says something suitably comforting. I run wailing through the house, keening like a banshee for my lost life...

Once upon a time I pretended to be a boy. I didn't particularly like boys, but I knew they got a better deal than the one I was in for. I felt it instinctively. I spent many nights crying, once I realized I was stuck with it. It felt like a prison sentence, femaleness. Mixed messages came through daily... You are beautiful. Don't get pregnant. Spying on Anne in her bedroom. Spying on her dancing alone with the mirror, my wild boy heart beating with fury at her growing breasts, so soft and heavy. The thought of their purpose, of babies sucking... I gradually—what?—gave up? No. I—felt strange. Or—separate. That's it. Fourteen, fifteen, must be the worst age on the planet. My friends were changing, seemed like strangers. I think it was Bob's girlfriend, she didn't like him playing music with me anymore. We were just friends. I never thought of him as other than friend. He turned—like a mask—one day a smile and the next he called me "slag"—I didn't even know what that meant.

Is that when it started?

Then. Dad lost his job when I was fifteen. He slipped up for a millisecond, and the gods ate him. We didn't talk about it. Off limits.

(Hands over her ears.) Please don't argue. Please don't get mad, Dad. Stop him, Mum. Why don't you stop him? ..."house full of damned women"? Is that what you think of us, Dad? Is that what you think of me?

I change schools. The first day, in September, I walk up three flights of stairs, and I almost pass out. I have a fever, a hundred and five. I walk along the corridors, watching everyone. It's like being unreal, invisible.

(Whispers.) Kelpie? ...Kelpie?

She curls into a small ball, watching, apart.

...If I sit here they won't notice. I blend into the grass and the rocks. It's cool under the bridge. Their skins are sweating. They'll never see me or smell me. It's amazing what they can't see, what they never notice.

It's all they can talk of. Sex and eating. Seems the same thing. Health class—who can draw the most realistic penis. Fits of giggling, passing notes. Films of women giving birth, all that blood and screaming. I begin skipping classes. The cafeteria—such a smell. Open mouths, red lips. Things always going into them. I am sickened, I feel ill. I sit under the stairs. Eat an apple. It sustains me. For days.

I pray, I am purified, lit from within—a pure cold flame, getting smaller and brighter, like St. Francis of Assisi.

I am quiet. I am obedient. I go into the world, I watch. I see many things. There is Greed, she's in every supermarket, in every mall, at every corner—with the children, clutching the groceries, can't wait to get home, send them out to play, open the ice cream, plunge the spoon, the big one that I always use, shove it in my mouth, cools my tongue, quenches my thirst, makes me hungry, eat it all right down to the bottom so they'll never know I bought it, no one will ever know—oh, god! There's Jealousy, her skin lightly green. She lives down the block. "You lucky thing. You're so skinny." As she eats a lettuce leaf, her eyes eat me. Sloth—he's my neighbour. He wants me to come in. He eyes me with pleasure. He reclines on his bed. "Lie with me, watch TV, you're too busy for your body." His father, though, it's him I fear. He is Lechery, and he's everywhere. He's on billboards, licking at the feet of the models in their wrappings, going into the back rooms of video stores, flicking his eyes up and down my body and not even aware; he is adding a notch to his belt; I slither out of his way, I slide around corners. But he enters the room like a green mist, he's also good at stealth; creeps into my ears and eyes and poisons my longings with old man murmurs.

She plays her ribs like a harp, as if before a mirror.

There are three more. The one who promises I can have it all. The one who tells me I'm not good enough. And the one who may be waiting outside my door to carve me into—something—which I am not and never was and never can be.

(*Startled.*) I'm busy, Mum. I'm fine, Mum. Please don't come in. My homework. Nothing. No, I'll fix my own supper. Yes, I will. I'll be down soon, ok?

Listens for her mother to leave, then begins to exercise.

Like a racehorse, turn myself into a muscled machine. Bones and sinew scraping together. Can't sit still, upside down, inside out. Play my bones like a harp and they sing to me. Constantly high, starvation does that. I have a mantra.

(*Sensuously.*) Brown sugar, one cup. Pure vanilla, one teaspoon. One large brown egg. Fold all together, beat. Pure flour, one cup, baking soda, one teaspoon, baking powder same thing, add to egg and sugar. Fold all together, beat. Chocolate chips, half cup, walnut pieces, half cup. Fold…together. 10 minutes warm oven, brown at edges, remove still warm!

Makes eighteen…

(*Sly.*) I know what's happened. I can even, sometimes, see it as others do. There's this woman, working at McDonald's? She has it too. She is so thin, but on her it looks revolting. I don't know how she does it. She has what I have, she must think as I do, and yet she works at a place which serves food, food that smells, rotten meat, people stuffing, fat children and greasy moustaches—

She holds her hand over her mouth, recovers.

She has white spittle at the corners of her mouth; it looks like she's rabid. She cleans the tables. She moves so fast, food all around her, smelt and untasted. What kind of will power does *that* take, eh? More than mine?

Today I sat with a freshly baked cookie. I won.

She exercises furiously.

Thin enough, there are choices. St. Joan on horseback, nothing to slow her, keep her home. To battle! She hears voices in her head, and they believe her. She dresses in man's armour, she rides to war. But she's caught and pulled from her kelpie. She throws herself from a tower trying to escape, they tie her to a pyre, and they cook and eat her flesh. Oh, yes, they do. Joan did not get away. I must not make any mistakes.

She suddenly is completely still, small, absent.

Mum? Save me? Dinner—a misery, a battleground where everyone's lost. I sit there, waiting, my face a blank. Anne wants to smash it. My mother eats for me, as once before she has—fed me— inside. Her eyes upon me, in such pain. *Why* don't you eat? *Why* won't you grow up? I'm deep and silent and cold, an artesian well—no divers, no equipment and data, no *any*thing will find the bottom. Search harder! Deeper! We are not children, we are not adults. We are chrysalis. We will be transformed! My family doctor, a nice old man who's given me lollipops since I was five. *He* doesn't know what to do. "How many calories have you taken in this morning? Yesterday? You know you're going to have to eat, you're going to have to stop this." He is wrong. We don't know. We are determined to win this war. He explains how serious it has become. Good, we think. Perhaps now you'll do something. What, we don't know. I bend over for a booster; the behind is the only place left with any flesh on it—but I'm working on that. "This is ridiculous, don't you realize you could DIE?" The words have been spoken, the gauntlet thrown down. "We'll have to begin to consider hospitalization. *(Pause.)* Did you hear me?" I'm not deaf, old man. I'm many other things but I am—NOT!—deaf. *(Whisper.)* I have been a shout in battle, I have been a raging stream.

I want to go back where I belong!

She paces, now hyper. She is speaking to a psychologist.

Because I don't *want* to sit down, ok?

I shouldn't be here. I don't want to talk to you. Because. I'm not stupid. I know all about the Second World War, you know. I've seen every picture in the school library. I've felt the trenches and the blood and the gas chambers and the pits. I've been buried in lime. I've been a Nazi in hiding. I know why whales can't give birth in captivity, and why Native North Americans die when they're incarcerated. I also know that the earth is almost completely destroyed and at the same time it's impossibly beautiful and it makes my heart—squeeze up.

Everyone's trying to protect me. They send me home from school; they think I scare people. And they send me to you, because they think I can talk to a stranger? It's too late, it's already in here. All this stuff, all these feelings, and images, all this all this—stuff!! *(She is banging her chest.)* I'm an old soul! You think you see "female," you see "girl"? But you're not seeing *me*, not the real me, and I'll tell you what I think—

—I think it's too late, the moment you're born. You're embarked, whether you want to be or not. You didn't ask to be. It was forced on you. And I need to know. I have to decide. Whether it's going to be worth it, of course!

Or not.

She "watches" him pass by. Sly.

I know what he's after, my shrink. He waits, hoping for miracles. Mother blame, father blame. He thinks it's easy. He's a stupid man. I've been going two years, for our game of hide and seek. He waits, Kleenex box ready—if only she'd cry, we could move forward. I can smell manipulation a mile away—I turn to stone. He gets Anne to come with me, see if that might help. Ha! Poor Anne. Always worried about what people think, so terrified she'll have an original thought.

One summer, when I was ten? We're visiting friends in B.C.—and Anne's, like—fourteen?—she gets into a heated love-thing with a pimply guy in black leather and a motorcycle—and he follows us all the way back across the continent! Imagine some Hell's Angel guy, in *our* family? Sitting around the Christmas table, him eating his turkey with his fingers or something, trying to come up with things to talk about. "How's it hangin', Tom? And hey, how about them Oilers?" He finally cools off around Kenora, disappears. Anne pouts for a while, then starts at her new school, and off she goes again, boys central. No wonder my parents are worried. "They're only after one thing, Sarah." Hey, don't worry. Totally opposite! Aren't you glad? Isn't this better? See how good I am? I couldn't care less about the opposite sex. Or even the same sex. Aren't you proud of me now?

...Dad? Why do you say that, they're only after one thing? You'd only say that if it's true for you.

Is it true—for you?

...Kelpie? Hello, boy... Please say hello, boy.

> *She hears Kelpie.*

—Do you hear that? You didn't hear that? They all look at me. Anne rolls her eyes. I wait till I'm alone.

...Like this? I take my skin and twist till I cry. I would cut it off if I could. But Kelpie doesn't tell me to go that far.

I need help with the hard things, Kelpie... You promise? I need you... I'm glad.

> *Pause. She remembers.*

...Tod. My sister's boyfriend. Anne and Tod...

Middle of winter. Dining room. This is before. I'm young, I still eat my dinner. Kelpie lurking outside. Anne is eighteen, I'm— fourteen. Anne comes in—she's going to a dance. My father stands, holds out his arms, she twirls into them. He laughs, kisses her forehead.

"She's a woman! Catherine, why didn't we notice? Sarah, isn't your sister beautiful?"

Anne is proud. She looks at me. I look at him. My father's face is white. He's seen a ghost. Can I go, too?

"Of course not."

Why not?

"You're too young."

For what? I want to go out at night, that's all. *She's* going out.

"She's with Tod."

What does that have to do with it?

"She's with a man. A young girl by herself—for heaven's sake, Sarah, don't be stupid intentionally."

A white light explodes in my head, washes through my blood like ice—So lock up the men! My mother looks frightened. My father's turned to stone.—And you shouldn't let her go out with Tod if you're so afraid of her getting pregnant, Mum. He grabbed me in the hall last week and stuck his tongue down my throat! In our house! While you were sitting in the living room!

Anne's face, splinters of broken glass, my mother's hands fluttering, and my father—what is he doing?—he takes me by the shoulders.

"Sarah. Don't be a fool—"

"Thomas." My mother's warning voice.

Anne's mouth opens. She screams, "You lying little—!" She runs at me. Then—I am pushed into the chair.

I feel bound! Held down! I hear words—"jealous"—"wants attention"—"soon grow up"—Don't want your stupid boyfriend! Want to tell you! Don't you hear me? Don't you care what he did?

"Tod would never—"

My mother hovers. Anne's nails bite into my arm.

My father tries to—what?—joke? "—Irish gods, Sarah. Be careful what you wish for. You just might get it!"

I twist and squirm. It's not funny! I'm in danger. It's not safe! Kelpie!

"Oh, for heaven's sake, Catherine, do something with your daughter. I give up!" He lets go of me, he pushes my chair—it feels like revulsion.

Ice fills my ears, my mouth... You don't believe me. You think I lie. You don't believe what is true. Tod's slug-like tongue down my throat.

I try to explain. I follow him into the kitchen. He's getting ice for his drink. "You were right, Dad. They *are* only after one thing." His face contorts. Is it pain? You believe me, don't you? "I don't—know what to believe. Oh, god, Catherine, get them away from me, I—" We are struggling. Ice from the tray goes flying, and I think he has—what? Hit me? Can't be. He is desperate. I am frightened. He loves me. I adore him!—I don't understand anything!

Is *that* when it started?

...I wake, go downstairs. Dad at the table with a drink, fourth or fifth gin and tonic; you never sleep, we none of us sleep, so aware of each other in this house. Trying to numb yourself and us out of your mind, so filled with despair that we don't exist—why do you leave us? What did we do wrong? What can I do right?

Kelpie!

...I am in the waiting room, they are behind a screen. It's as if I'm not there, as if, as I get smaller, I am shrinking out of sight.

—"I'm sorry, Mr. O'Brien, but your daughter's not responding to treatment. In fact, she's losing ground fast. I'm quite worried."

"But I don't understand. She's got her own shelf in the kitchen. We let her fix the food she wants."

"She's adept at fooling you—at fooling herself. Have you seen her in a swim suit lately?"

"She doesn't come to the pool with us anymore."

"The psychologist tells me they're not making any progress."

"Is that *her* fault? *He's* the doctor, for god's sake!"

"Mr. O'Brien, I understand you're going through a tough time—"

"What the hell do you mean?"

"I'm sure the loss of employment—"

"How dare you! How dare you!"

"The pressures parental figures are under reflect on the psyche of—"

…Muuuuuummm!

"—I know you're fine, Sarah. Your father and I know you're strong. You're extremely strong. But we're frightened. Listen, look, I can put my finger and thumb together round your arm—come on, sweetheart, it's too much. You need help. Just for a few days. Just till you stabilize."

I remember—

Finger and thumb together. You can see into Tir na n'Og through the fairy ring.

And what's in there?

Anything you want. It's eternity.

And what's eternity?

A wish never to leave.

Kelpie? Come. Come. Now. *(Fierce):* Now!

We drive for several hours. Anne is with us. She's living with Tod now. We don't speak of him. This "hospital"—a large piece of property, lots of trees. That's nice. The place itself, the building, and the smell. Like boiled bedpans, or deathrags. They leave me here. Of course I'll be fine, goodbye, see you soon. Some of the nurses are nuns. Every morning, a senior doctor looks in on me, trailed by hungry interns. Mostly men. One woman. She doesn't interest me; she wants too much to be liked, to be accepted. Pathetic. I am different. They've never seen anyone like me. I am a new creation. They come along at 8:00 a.m. like a flock of seagulls. I float up to the ceiling. They lift my hospital gown above my ribcage—sheet draping my hips—crowd round, one after another, gently poking my enlarged spleen. They seem thrilled. They chatter like magpies. I'm not there. I am watching myself from the ceiling, a crowd of white coats around a wasted body in a bed; one day, one day, I'll have the key and I'll be gone.

There's a pecking order, right? Fatties at the bottom, they're the plebs. Can't stop eating till their stomachs are stapled shut. Pathetic, eh? Next up the evolutionary ladder are bulimics—they are secretive, ashamed. They admire the anorexics. But they can't do it. Instead they vomit; comfort themselves with food, then throw it back up. The acid rots their teeth out. And it's wasteful: think of all the starving peoples of the world. No one has to say it; they think it, they know it. They punish themselves every single day. Then, like a shining light, come the anorexics, the admired ones. Thoroughbreds, aristocrats. They hear voices, sit still for hours at a time, or *explode* screaming and running. Extremely temperamental. They're the ones that die. It's quite romantic. Like consumptives, pre-Raphaelite Ophelias, floating down the river.

They don't get reproached with wasting food, though. Think of that.

(*Responding to a nurse.*) Good morning, Sister. *We* are both fine thank you. Humour's to be expected, I'm reading Lenny Bruce— (*As her book is pulled away.*) Hey, that's mine! Too late now. It's in here... No. No movement at all. Tragic, but true. I think I'm going to blow up. Actually, I'm serious. I'm in a lot of pain. I'm going to explode! It doesn't make sense to stuff more in when it's all still sitting there, don't you understand, you stupid cow!

(*Beat. Responding to a doctor.*) No, I wasn't feeling charitable this morning, but Sister Isobel was provoking me! Oh, really? Well, (*She imitates him.*) "I think you'll find" she gets a sadistic pleasure

out of it, talking about bowel movements when she knows I can't
stand it! I *don't* think the world is out to get me. I— They won't let
me take a bath—it's the only way I can get warm, and when I'm in
the tub, they're constantly looking in. I can't lock the door to keep
them from staring. I'm—! *(She listens.)* Privacy. To take my bath.
Fine.

Alone, at last. I've craved it, I've fought for it—I cry with hunger.
Sit up for hours in the dark and cry, silently, mouth open. The food
from each day's meals lying squashed and rotting under my
mattress. They don't know. They think I'm obeying. They can't
figure out why I'm not gaining weight—I'm losing it faster. You'd
better hurry up, you morons! Don't you know anything? Can't you
hear me? It takes them two weeks before the smell from my bed
alerts them to what I am doing. They probably think it's my breath,
so it takes them longer to notice. I've lost another ten pounds.

One day, walking, I come upon a nun. They don't wear habits, but
you can always tell. The big serious cross round their necks kind of
gives them away. I tower over this nun. I like the feeling.

"You're Sarah. I've heard of you."

Like a racehorse, everyone is betting on my chances. Including me.

She is Sister Mary Simon. Why are you a nun?

"I am a nun out of choice. Just as you are thin out of choice. Makes
sense?"

(Wary.) I guess so.

"Let's walk, shall we?"

She tells me about herself. I don't ask, don't say anything, but she
is undeterred. Her mother, Helen, was English. Married a
graduate student from Calcutta, in 1910. Helen was ostracized—
by friends, by family. Her husband lost his scholarships, had to go
back to India. They promised to be together as soon as they could.
It was a question of money. Helen never heard from him again. She
discovered she was pregnant. A terrible—complication. One day
she met a woman who was also alone, but not afraid, who was out

in the world, doing. So Helen also joined the Women's Social and Political Union, became a suffragette.

Suffragette. What's that?

Sister Mary Simon sends me to the hospital library. I read. These are my people! The Pankhursts, Lady Lytton. They wanted the vote. They broke windows, held rallies, and were taken to prison. They'd decided not to eat, that their bodies were the last bastions of power. They were force fed, then released. And they did it again. And there were others!—Mahatma Gandhi, Bobby Sands, Simone Weill—the audacity! The silent "take notice!" It's protest, it's political! I thought I was alone! "Yes, but, Sarah," she says, "what are you striking *for*? Can you tell me? What do *you* want?" I put my hands over my ears, but—again she draws me on.

She was born, christened Suna in 1911. It means light after darkness.

That is so beautiful! Suna... What happened to Helen then? And where was your father?

Helen became a hunger-striker. Suna was raised in several different homes, by several different women during those years, depending which of them was in or out of prison at any one time. She tells of a memory—probably her first memory at age two or three—of her mother, pale and dirty, coming down a garden pathway leaning on the arms of two other women. That day, Helen had received a telegram. On her husband's journey home to Calcutta, a dissident had run amok through a crowd at a train station, firing bullets. Only one had died.

Your *father*? ...I hear roaring.

"Sarah? Look at me. What is happening?"

I don't know. It stinks!

"Yes, I know, life stinks. It is also hard. But the opposite is death. You don't wish that do you? *Do* you?"

Maybe.

"You're asking for help."

No, I'm not.

"I recognize it."

No, you *don't*! I feel sick! What's going to happen to me?

"That's up to you, isn't it? The choices you make."

I can't do anything, you're crazy. I'm stuck in this—box, I—

"Oh, Sarah, you are not quite letting yourself see the other side. You have to *look* for it, and fight for it, but it *is* there."

She makes me think, all the time, think so hard. She never coddles me, or calls me stupid. She never pretends to feel anything for me that isn't real. I see a tiny hole back into the real world.

"The suffragettes were women who wanted a voice, a share in shaping the world and their own lives. You've read the facts, Sarah, but the truth is this: a hunger strike is a gamble. The striker must rely on the humanity of her jailors. What if they refuse to back down? What if they don't understand the importance of her demand? Her goal must be clear—give me the vote, and I will eat. So, here we are. What are you demanding of me? Do you see what I'm asking? What do we need to give you to allow you to give up your hunger strike?"

My mind a blank. The words spinning around in it. It had seemed like a gift, to know about suffragettes. Why must she keep going on and on? I don't want to know *why* women stopped eating at the beginning of the last century, I just want to know *how*.

"Sarah. Turn it around. What do you *want*?"

To... I don't know! A roaring in my ears—shut up! I am evil. Don't say anything. Give nothing away! I push through, I shove: To—have a choice?—a *real* choice. Something more? Something—*else*?

No trumpet sounds. No apocalypse begins. Instead, her calm voice goes on. My heart begins to settle as I hear syllables and vowels—only later do I make sense of them:

"—reasonable to me. There are a million ways to live a life, there is no pattern fixed in stone. We must find choices, then. And we'll talk."

I can't. I have to—

"You don't have to do anything."

I have nothing to say.

"You need practice. You can practice with me. Of course, not all the time, that would be a strain for us both. We'll get out in the world— we'll listen to music—and look at art—find what's been uplifting through the centuries, as *well* as the holocausts. You want knowledge, you must be wide-ranging."

"Will it be *my* knowledge?"

"Yes."

"Will it be safe?"

—and at that she would always laugh. "Nothing is safe, Sarah. You don't want me to lie to you. You are here for many reasons, but the main one is you need love—without sorrow, without competition, and not bound up in guilt or pain. This is not easy to find, or to give, until you can articulate it to yourself. You are making the first steps."

Pause.

The family visits often. My parents seem happier. Because *I* am gone. On their own again, grownups and lovers together. Maybe I *am* jealous. It's very strange between Anne and I. She has a job at a record store, taunts me with it.

"I've broken up with Tod—"

The jerk.

"—with Tod. And I'm moving to my own place. It's what I want. Brian from the store is going to help me move."

Brian? Warning bells sound.

"Yeah."

From the store?

"You're so paranoid, Sarah. What's wrong with that?"

I don't know, I—

"Want to know something else, little Miss Purity? We screw."

Anne! You said he's married! His wife's going to have a baby!

"Yeah, so? Oh, what do you know about it? You don't have a clue."

She's right, I don't. And I don't want to! I picture his wife, giving birth, feet in stirrups, surrounded by strangers, and where is he? Where's Brian? Deep inside Anne, my sister enjoying it, lust and betrayal on and on and…on.

They have to take her away. I am hitting her with my fists. They give me tranquilizers. That night, I hear Kelpie outside on the grounds. I rush to the window, and there—there!—I knock on the glass. I am pounding on the glass! Kelpie is whinnying, galloping around. Kelpie's back is naked, waiting for me. I want to be on it. I am ready to go! To Tir na n'Og! Wait, don't go yet. Let me *be* you again!—I love you—I'm your boy! He spins away, hooves flashing, disappearing forever? I break the window with my fists, fall onto the grass below, I am crazy, covered in blood and—start running, running—behind me in white, coats flapping, they follow…

> *After this physical re-enactment of the breaking of the window, etc., Sarah is now once again still, detached, as if observing herself from the outside.*

They start force-feeding me. There's no euphemistic way to put it. Forced. Feeding. The first time I don't understand. I just say, as usual, I'm not hungry. The doctor gives me a quick look-over— listens to my heart, takes my pulse. Two more nurses come in. They look smug. One of them's Sister Isobel, the one I've called a fat cow. Two of them hold my arms, one my head, one my feet. My heart starts to race. Shut my mouth, clench my teeth. The doctor tells me to open my mouth. *(She shakes her head.)* He says he'll use a steel gag, which won't hurt if I obey him and open my mouth. *(Again.)* He leans on my knees as he tries to get me to do what he wants. It hurts. He says if I resist they'll have to feed me through the nose. I'm frightened, and he senses it; he gets the gag between my teeth and he fastens the screws wide open, much wider than my mouth would normally go. Then they put a tube down my throat—at least four feet long. I keep choking, my raw throat closing around the tube. At last it's in. Water is running from my eyes. They pour the food in fast. As soon as it reaches my stomach I need to vomit—it comes up around the tube and all over myself and them... It seems a long time before they take the tube out. Everyone leaves. It's over an hour before they let me take my bath. I'm seventeen years old.

After that? After my "relapse"? I fight it more. They "feed" me through my nose. Over and over. Like the suffragettes, I call to me in my cell, call myself to bravery, I summon him to me—no surrender. No surrender, no surrender, no surrender!

And I'm there.

> *She is Kelpie. She snorts, tosses her head. The following is very physical.*

There's a crow on my head, moss and muck in my nose. I'm in the bog. They say it will kill me, but I'll never die. On the bad days— keep my nostrils above the surface, my legs below me swimming. Eyes far-seeing—with a film upon them that sees only life.

On the good days, I'm on the turf. I'm up and moving like the wind. I work at it. Body good, stomach flat and hard, rippled ribs, long thighs. And I'm running, breath coming through me, pumping breath, bellows ribs going in, going out—they won't fail me, they are strong and they're sure. Crow above me, flying, and I snort, toss my neck. Plunge halt. And he's there. Lower my head. Breath goes in, goes out. Little boy. He sees me, beautiful—human harp singing out, crying out. Can't resist, either one of us. Hello, boy. I've learned my manners, dip my knees for him. Feel his thighs on my back. His hot skin against mine. While I'm strong, while I've got him, never rest, always flying, pumping breath, drumming hooves. It is wonderful—but he shouldn't, no, he

shouldn't, turn me westward, turn me waterward!—sea salt in my
nostrils calls me back. Running faster, crow swoops lower, pecks
my ears—he is frightened. Hold on tight, boy, round my neck. I
can't stop for you nor for anyone. Can't stop a kelpie on the moor,
on the flat, fit and able. One sniff of water and your life's not worth
a tinker's damn, for I'll drown you sure as hell and it's a long—
way—down. Boy.

She comes to rest, panting. Then sings.

What did you learn there,
under the trees,
where the sound of the wind
is the surge of hidden seas
and the dreaming trees murmur
in a tongue you dare not speak
and the song of the blackbird
masks the murdered, ravaged shriek.

…There was a time when the girl saw no one, no family, no friends.
Immured. She's a good girl and takes her forcefeeding like a man.
A dark love moves her heart muscles.

She refuses to see Suna for weeks at a time. Suna walks on,
unperturbed. The girl follows at a distance, holds debates with the
nun in her head. You are not a nun out of choice. "Neither are you
thin out of choice." What are you talking about? Of course I am. "I
am a nun because of a concatenation of circumstances when I was
young. We have been branded by the times we are living in. I love
God, and humankind—and you, sometimes, Sarah." The girl is
furious.

Sarah becomes the Kelpie suddenly. She snorts.

What would *you* know of life, or of love? You're a NUN! You've
never had to face the world. You wander around here like a holy
brown oracle—no sex, no pain. You don't have to give birth or be
expected to love someone their whole long and *ugly* life through—
you don't have to pretend to feel passion when all you want is to be
left ALONE!—leave me ALONE!

Just then, in the hospital library, the girl finds a ballad from the Middle Ages—"The Singing Bones." Two sisters are walking by a river. The elder pushes the younger into the water, holds her under until she drowns. Her body washes up into a millpond, and a harper comes upon it, pulls the body from a weir. The harper thinks her beautiful, like Ophelia. Nec-rOphelia. He turns the corpse into a harp. The girl imagines the details. He slits open her chest, peels back her skin, rips out her organs, discards the parts he does not need. He scalps her and strings the breastbone with her own hair. He turns her finger bones into tuning pegs. *He* creates the instrument. *He* makes it possible for her to sing. She waits for him to animate her, sings *his* songs. How can she be free? The girl is horrified. She rejects this story! Then...then!

Sarah's energy is building, focused.

The girl is walking, outside, by the river. She feels powerful; she weighs seventy-five pounds. Someone is with her. Her sister. Anne. She wants to know what's going on, the girl is getting too strange.

(*Looks her sister up and down.*) Promise not to tell. With your life. And I mean it.

The sister looks funny, then agrees.

I...love someone. We're going away.

Her lip goes into its curl. The girl's nostrils begin to flare, her legs to tingle.

"Just a minute. Who is this guy, anyway? Where'd he come from?"

How do you know it's a man?

"Very funny."

It could be a woman. Or anything, why not?

"You're such a little show-off. It's driving me nuts, Sarah!"

(*Ugly, from the depths, like the Kelpie:*) GO AWAY, PIG! YOU'RE A BIG FAT PIG!

First real communion. She blinks, then speaks carefully:

"The things you say are crazy, Sarah. Life's not a fairy tale, you know."

Big sister, back in charge. The girl likes the other one better, wants that one back.

I'm pared down. This is me. If you don't like it, then go AWAY!

The bared face is back, and she loves it! "I hate you—you're not my sister—" and she pushes the girl into the water. The river's reedy— they run, screaming, through the water and the reeds—she catches the girl, grabs her hair—she pushes my face into the mud at the bottom of the river. And holds me there! *(Laughing.)* I'm going back!

       Gasping:

Suddenly! Ripped away. Pulled up and out, I am choking, eyes blurred with mud. I hear a voice, very angry—

"I could—have your hide!"

It is Suna. She is here. I am glad! She will make my sister pay!

"What do you think you're doing, Sarah? You must take everything too far. This is all romantic to you, isn't it? *Isn't* it?"

Something is wrong. I feel her real fingers clenched into my real arm. I hate it! Her eyes are blazing. It is wicked, wicked—to treat me this way. I will show her, I will—

—break free, kick my feet. Suna falls, flailing. He is there, he is calling me—Wait for me, I'm coming! I am under the water again. I grab onto reeds, force myself down. I see him. There he is—I am here, Kelpie! He is coming closer. I will be Kelpie forever!

(Kelpie's voice:) …Don't think. Just come, boy. It's beautiful, it's what you want. …Forget them. Die for me, Sarah.

—Swirls of churned mud part at the very last moment, like the red sea and THERE—! No muscle, no bellows harp, no!—no life in its

eyes. A skeleton, a ghoul, in its underworld! Empty sockets—its
mane envelops me, tangles around my face, my arms; flesh hangs
from bones—he is hideous! He will tune my finger pegs, he will rip
my human harp—

Gasping, her body taking her back to the surface—

Suddenly—I'm an animal being, needing to LIVE—it will not be
silenced, it will not OBEY—it ROARS to the surface—

—My BODY!

Sound of rain. Sarah very still.

...What is real? This is real. Lying on my back on the bank. Suna is
giving me the kiss of life. Her mouth on mine, filling me with air.
She is really here, this is really happening. We are both soaking wet
and covered in mud from the bottom of the river. We are panting.
It is raining—needles on my skin—air in my lungs, breath goes in,
goes out—human harp, singing out, crying out... Hold on to me.
She will not let me go—and I come back. I come back from being
away. Body, soul. On solid ground. For the first time in three years.

She sings.

> What did you find there
> that so quietly you go?
> Was it an older secret
> than the one you sought to know?
> Laughing you came in
> as bright as the day
> and your childhood walked with you
> but alone you came away.

Anne wasn't there that day. It was all me. We have a good girl self
that keeps us quiet—a bigger sister, keeps us down. That's what
Suna said. I reconnected with my body. And little by little, I got
better. The suffragettes had won the vote and went on with their
lives—and not in prison. Hunger striking is a tool, not the end in
itself—is that right? Suna was always there, no judgement. No
need to achieve or impress, just hear me; *all* of me, even the not so
nice bits.

Fact is, I was no Suna for you, Katie.

What were you thinking, that day in the cafeteria? Were you testing the ground, trying to come back? Sure that if you took it slowly, you could do it, you could return. But it happens so fast, that one false move—and…it's over, Katie.

I keep thinking about your story, "The Singing Bones." What *you'd* done with the myth. You…turned it around. Gave the younger sister choice—made her swim away, return to the elements, right down to the bone, then sing her own truth. You were so close!

…I'm so scared. Of making mistakes. Of you—little fish. Fathers, mothers—I am not so brave. I can't cope with a daughter, have something go wrong. Watch her turn into me, see her dying in a cafeteria, unable to live…

When my father was dying, and we were alone, he said, "I loved you all, as much as I knew how. I was eaten by the gods." There was a silence, then he frowned, shook his head. "No. I *let* myself be eaten." *(Remembering, puzzled.)* He said something else—"Don't fear it." The next day he died.

I went to Ireland then—I was compelled—to a place near Kilkenny. Five miles from where he'd grown up, where he'd romped and played. There was a creek and I followed—it began to rain, then cleared up—and suddenly…there it is—

And in her mind, she is there, it is present, it is now.

The most remarkable stone. Five feet tall, one foot thick—a hole in the centre, big enough to pass a body through. Pass a child through this ring, holding on to it tight so it can't slip away, and it will always be well, that's the belief. "Finger and thumb, in a circle, see into Tir na n'Og." I see your boy face pressed to the hole in the stone, searching, searching. I am so much your child! …A cool hand slips into mine. I stay very still. I thought he'd meant death, Katie. But no—it was life. Don't fear *life*.

"You're right."

Then—?

"Come a bit farther. Come through. We can do it."

Is it safe?

I don't know.

Is it…worth it?

Yes. Come on.

And I step close to the hole in the stone. We take turns—she looks back at what she's left behind, and I help her. I look forward, into what might be, and she helps me. And we both catch a glimpse of eternity, long enough to do us. I fall on my back in the long, mist-drenched grass. Everything is green and weeping. My hands are on my body, and I give myself over. I welcome this little fish inside—

> *Sarah's hands are on her belly. The revelation of acceptance sits in this moment, and the Katie she now speaks to is inside herself.*

Hi, Katie.

"Hi."

END

Printed in March 1999 by

VEILLEUX
ON DEMAND PRINTING INC.

in Longueuil, Quebec